PRAISE FOR UNBREAKABLE US

Your primary relationship is with yourself, so if you wish to have glorious connections with others, start by working on yourself. Here is a brilliant primer to help you do just that. This is the wise and practical guide that you need to heal your relationship with yourself, so that you can create fulfilling relationships with others. Joëlle is an insightful facilitator who will inspire you on your journey of inner healing, self-discovery, and reclaiming.

— SHERI WINSTON, WHOLISTIC SEXUALITY
TEACHER, AUTHOR OF WOMEN'S ANATOMY OF
AROUSAL, AND FOUNDER OF THE
INTIMATE ARTS CENTER

In *Unbreakable Us*, Lydon invites us into a courageous exploration of what we truly want when we search for love and then acts as a sherpa to help us navigate the path to find it.

— KAT KOPPETT, CEO, KOPPETT, AND AUTHOR OF
TRAINING TO IMAGINE AND *THE FACILITATION
ADVANTAGE*

I was blown away by Joëlle's authenticity, honesty, and wisdom [in *Unbreakable Us*]. She is someone who has transformed her life in the process of finding and understanding love and now offers the wisdom gained from experience to those of us still struggling in this domain. If you want to succeed in creating a loving relationship, this book is the place to begin and end your search.

— MICHAEL LEE, MA, FOUNDER OF PHOENIX RISING YOGA THERAPY AND AUTHOR OF *TURN STRESS INTO BLISS*

Reading *Unbreakable Us* was like being handed a lantern while walking through the dark forest of love. I've watched Joëlle live her love courageously and out loud—and now, through these pages, she shows the rest of us how. Her raw truth-telling, wisdom, and practical guidance helped me soften my defenses and open my heart in ways I didn't know I needed. Because of Joëlle—and this extraordinary book—I've found the courage to seek and receive lasting love in my own life. This isn't just a book. It's a revolution of the heart.

As a teacher and guide to women on the path of embodied healing and empowerment, I will be sharing *Unbreakable Us* with the community of women I serve. It is a powerful resource for any woman ready to remove the barriers to love and reclaim the fullness of who she truly is.

— DEBORAH KERN, PHD, FOUNDER OF PRANASHAKTI™ AND SACRED FEMININE MENTOR

Joëlle Lydon presents a unique perspective in her book *Unbreakable Us* on what it takes to thrive in relationships in these crazy, modern times. This book is a must-read for anyone who desires, at the end of the day, a sense of peace, a sense of self-respect, and a sense of hope for the future.

— HEATHER DOMINICK, AUTHOR OF *DIFFERENT: HOW TO REDUCE OVERWHELM AND INCREASE INCOME AS A HIGHLY SENSITIVE PERSON,* AND FOUNDER OF BUSINESS MIRACLES

Joëlle has given us an interactive map, and a way to reignite our relationship with the very best kind of LOVE: Self, whole being love, ensuring that the WE we share is inclusive of the most important relationship—the one we have with ourselves!

— DEBBIE ROSAS, FOUNDER OF THE NIA TECHNIQUE

Brilliant! Raw! Candid! Inspirational! Joëlle has created a pathway for self-discovery in love and a gentle reminder that, through our interconnectedness, you don't have to journey alone. From learning to draw a line in the sand to giving grace when needed to move forward in love, I was riveted by every word. Anyone looking for transformation in the love arena needs a copy of this book on their shelf.

— JANET TANGUAY, CEO OF THE HAMMOCK WAY OF LIFE LLC

Using courageous self-revelations, practical exercises, and an authentic understanding of the difficult task ahead, this book is an excellent resource for achieving the satisfying life you have longed for and deserve. Loved the book and can't wait to read the rest! Joëlle is such a special person.

— DONNA BRENT, PSYD, LICENSED PSYCHOLOGIST
SPECIALIZING IN COMPLEX POST-TRAUMATIC
STRESS DISORDER

What a gift! *Unbreakable Us* is more than a book—it's a wise, inspiring, and deeply practical wayfinder for love. Joëlle leads with clarity, compassion, and hard-won wisdom, demystifying the inner path to connection. If you're hungry for deeper love and lasting transformation, start here. I've read hundreds of books on love—this is the best.

— EDI PASALIS, MBA, MTS, CERTIFIED MENOPAUSE
COACHING SPECIALIST

Joëlle's courageous transparency reminds us that the key to more loving relationships begins with transforming our relationship to love. This is way more than a book—it's a soul-centered guide on creating happier, healthier, and more fulfilling partnerships.

— DONNA OTMANI, SOUL-CENTERED PROFESSIONAL
LIFE COACH AND FOUNDER OF THE INRWRK

Unbreakable Us quickly gets to the heart of the matter and is a game-changer in the work—and manifestation—of love.

— LIZ LINDER, OWNER, LIZ LINDER
PHOTOGRAPHY, INC.

If you're ready to walk the deeper path to finding your power to create the relationships you feel deep in your heart you desire and deserve, Joëlle Lydon is a worthy and wise guide. She's walked the talk and lived the experience to find and bring forth practical and inspiring wisdom, not just more tips and tricks. You can trust the work and words she's put into this book.

— CHRISTINE ARYLO, MBA LEADERSHIP ADVISOR,
AND AUTHOR OF *OVERWHELMED AND OVER IT*

[*Unbreakable Us*] provoked quiet self-reflection and a gentle challenge to look at love with a new perspective. What I especially appreciate is that this isn't just a book of ideas—it's a guide to take action. The inclusion of elements like the Love Lab Challenges and Creative Edge Expressions makes the book feel alive and participatory. I felt invited into active pursuit of the unbreakable love I think we all long for, and sometimes, feel bewildered about how to achieve.

— CLARE A. MONTEAU, PH.D., CONSULTANT AND
FACILITATOR OF SYSTEMIC TRANSFORMATION

This book is mind-blowing! A radically different approach that will transform all the ways you love, lead, and relate!

— JESSICA PROCINI, FOUNDER AND LEADER,
ESCAPE FROM EMOTIONAL EATING®

Unbreakable Us is more than a memoir—it's a lush, living ecosystem of healing and wisdom. Through Joëlle's heart-led storytelling and creative practices, we're invited to explore love as a living system: Tender, complex, and wildly transformative. This is a book for seekers and believers alike—those ready to conspire with curiosity, to dance in embodied truth, and to root deeply into the sacred soil of connection, where conscious love becomes the seed of a more beautiful world.

— ALLIE MIDDLETON, COMMISSIONED AUTHOR AND FOUNDER

Let Joëlle Lydon guide you on a journey of inner and outer discovery. This relationship roadmap is your wayfinding companion to reclaiming the love, intimacy, and connection you desire … and deserve. There is no better book to support you in creating lasting love. Give yourself this gem; highly recommended!

— RENEE PETERSON TRUDEAU, CATALYST/RETREAT FACILITATOR AND AUTHOR OF *THE MOTHER'S GUIDE TO SELF-RENEWAL: HOW TO RECLAIM, REJUVENATE AND RE-BALANCE YOUR LIFE*

If you're successful in your work but struggling in love, Joëlle shines a light on the hidden patterns that hold smart, capable women, like you, back in their relationships. Unbreakable Us is honest, empowering, and shows you how to create the deep connection your heart—and your soul—truly craves.

— BARBARA HUSON, FINANCIAL THERAPIST, WEALTH COACH, AND AUTHOR OF *REWIRE FOR WEALTH: THREE STEPS ANY WOMAN CAN TAKE TO PROGRAM HER BRAIN FOR FINANCIAL SUCCESS*

UNBREAKABLE US

UNBREAKABLE US

REMOVING THE BARRIERS TO LOVE

JOËLLE LYDON

HIGHLANDER
PRESS

ISBN: 978-1-956442-62-5
Ebook ISBN: 978-1-956442-63-2
Library of Congress: Applied For.

Published by Highlander Press
501 W. University Pkwy, Ste. B2
Baltimore, MD 21210

Cover design: Lisa Hromada
Editor: Deborah Kevin
Author photo: Andrew Elder

CONTENTS

Part IV
GROWING TOGETHER (AND FLOURISHING)

For my parents, Antony and Gwynne,
with gratitude for the opportunity to learn to find home.

For my husband, Matthew, my legendary affair.
I still love you, and I'll never take it back.

For my son, Liam, my first true love.
Being your mother is the greatest honor of my life.

And for all those still searching, still believing—may you come to know that love
is not only possible, it's the sacred ground from which a better world begins.

INTRODUCTION

> *Until you make the unconscious conscious, it will dictate your life and you will call it fate.*
>
> — CARL JUNG

The first time I tried to end my life, I was twelve years old. In the attic with my father's tie and a stool, I strung the noose around my neck with the determination only a pre-teen can summon, fueled by a defiant, *"You'll be sorry."*

The tie didn't hold. I came crashing to the floor, flooded with shame for failing even at this. Shame at my own perceived stupidity. While simultaneously feeling relief—no one was there to witness my humiliation and pour ridicule over it.

Had you told me then I'd grow up to be a relationship coach or write a book on love and connection, I would not have believed you.

My experience with relationships was that they were challenging. They always felt like an enigma to me. I watched others move fluidly through them with ease—talking, joking, laughing, touching—while I saw myself as an outsider, unable to find my way in. There was a veil between me and the world of connection, one I could feel but neither see nor penetrate. That sense of isolation and disenfranchisement haunted me for decades, feeding depression and suicidal ideation.

My formative years were steeped in familial turbulence: alcoholism, neglect, as well as emotional and physical abuse. At sixteen, expelled from the French Lycée I attended, I was sent across the ocean to live with my American aunt. That exile set me on a path that led me straight to a husband who, though new in name, carried similar wounds. A man who, like my family before him, would reinforce the lessons of unworthiness I had already internalized about myself.

The relationship and marriage lasted sixteen years.

Two years after leaving—still caught in the throes of court drama and battles—I fell in love for the first time. We blended our families, bought a home, and got a dog. Everything seemed so beautiful, like the start of something new and promising. And yet, eight years later, I found myself in another familiar place: unseen, unmet, misunderstood, yearning. While my then-partner was a huge improvement over my ex-husband, my own relational skills were still underdeveloped.

I struggled to express my true wants and desires, masking them in silence, acquiescence, and people-pleasing until alcohol loosened my tongue. Then, in a snap, the dam would break—unleashing a torrent of unspoken frustrations, disappointments, and rage. Mornings after were spent drowning in shame and regret.

The cycle of silence, desperation, frustration, disenfranchisement, and shame, coupled with the unrelenting pressures of the ongoing court battles with my ex, work, and life, spiraled me into a deep, dark place. I could hardly get out of bed. And, once again, began planning my suicide.

Then came November of 2008.

I woke up in a panic, dressed in a medical gown, on an institutional restraint bed with plastic mattress, the kind that needed special extra-long sheets you might remember if you ever stayed in a sleepaway camp. The kind that made crinkling sounds every time you moved. My belongings had been handed over to my then-partner for safekeeping. Dirty glass and metal bars on the windows obscured any view of the outside world. I remember standing barefoot on the cold linoleum floor in the hallway, trying to gather my thoughts.

Panic set in. I rushed to the dimly lit counter where a night nurse sat. Breathless, I pressed my hands on the counter and pleaded, "I don't belong here. How do I get out?"

The nurse looked at me patiently and smiled softly. "You can't leave. You're here until you're deemed safe enough to return home."

Safe?

"You have to get me out of here! This is NOT my life! I have to get out of here!" I screamed.

She calmly handed me a cup of water—one of those disposable ones that turn mushy if left too long—and a few small pills. Then, she placed a gentle arm around me, guiding me back to my room. There, I fell, unconscious, into a heavy, dense, foggy, and drug-induced sleep.

I had landed in a psychiatric ward, on suicide watch. Not the life I'd envisioned.

I held a master's degree, had been a Fulbright recipient, and had collected innumerable licenses, certifications, and awards. I was the daughter of a talented artist and United Nations civil servant who was an Oxford graduate. I was raised among other UN employees, ambassadors, politicians, journalists, musicians, and artists. I had survived a military *coup d'état*. And yet, there I was, stripped down to nothing, drowning in shame, locked in a psych ward.

Leading up to that moment, my life had become a whirlwind of self-created pressure. I worked full-time as a public-school teacher while mentoring student teachers as a part-time adjunct professor. I taught dance three evenings a week, ran product events for a networking business, conducted weekend workshops, presented at conferences, and juggled a never-ending to-do list—all while being a single mother, trapped in a seven-year battle with my ex. And my relationship—the one I had thought would finally bring me home to myself—was fast unraveling.

I was crumbling. Desperate. Overwhelmed. I was submerged in the belief that if I were just busy enough, accomplished enough, indispensable enough, then maybe, just maybe, I would be loved.

I didn't value myself. I didn't value my time.

Learning to love myself and allowing myself to be fully loved by another wasn't a singular event. It was a messy, painful, heart-wrenching evolution.

People say time is money. I say love is time:

- Time for yourself.
- Time to rest.
- Time to "be."
- Time to be nothing to nobody.
- Time to do what you love.
- Time to create.
- Time to be with be with those who matter.
- Time to serve in a way that nourishes you.
- Time to make a difference.

The next morning that November, I awoke once more in a panic. The never-ending list of to-dos and obligations flooding my mind— who was taking care of my son? The dog? The cats? How would I explain this to my friends, my colleagues, and my family? Powerlessness and shame wrapped themselves around me like a vice.

Standing in the hallway, paper slippers on my feet, surrounded by others who were lost in their own suffering, I reached a breaking point. I couldn't run. I couldn't leave. I couldn't call my partner to get me. I could do nothing … but surrender.

My inability to be clear, ask for what I needed, say "no" when necessary and "yes" when I desired it, and stand firm in my worth had led me to that point. I had danced around my own truth for over forty-five years, silencing myself, shapeshifting, and withholding instead of speaking up. I had repeatedly frozen when genuine honesty was required.

There is no breakthrough without a breakdown.

— TONY ROBBINS

In that moment of surrender, my life and my life's work began. That November was my turning point. While my circumstances were extreme, I've been doing this work long enough to know that the patterns that led me there are all too common. My journey—my research, my healing, my work, my legacy—exists so you don't have to end in a psychiatric ward to learn the lessons I did.

There is another way—one that begins with valuing yourself enough to invest in support, so you can learn to take up space unapologetically, sincerely ask for what you desire and require, stand fully in your worth, and claim love without sacrificing one iota of your life to receive it.

This is my invitation to you: Draw your line in the sand. Choose yourself. Now, before the breaking point, before the unraveling.

Because love—real love—begins and ends with you.

HOW TO USE THIS BOOK

The real voyage of discovery consists not in seeking new land-scapes, but in having new eyes.

— MARCEL PROUST

This book is meant to serve as your relationship road map. It's designed to help you locate where you are in the journey and guide you toward what's next.

Imagine being lost in a massive mall searching for H&M. You wander past a sea of storefronts until you finally spot a glowing kiosk that says, *"You are here."* Suddenly, everything makes more sense. You can see where you are, where you want to go, and how to get there.

That's exactly what this book is meant to be: your wayfinding companion. The steady arrow pointing to *"You are here,"* illuminating the next step toward the love, connection, and intimacy you've been seeking.

What you won't find here are quick fixes, short-term strategies, or anything resembling a one-size-fits-all solution. There are plenty of books and programs like that out in the world. You've probably tried more than a few. If they had worked you wouldn't be here, flipping through these pages, wondering what it *really* takes to create the kind of love that lasts.

What you will find here is something different: a path to deep healing. A soul-level transformation rooted in truth, intention, and lived experience. It's the kind of work that takes time, courage, and, most importantly, your ongoing willingness to participate in your transformation.

I work with those who struggle with knowing HOW to make this happen. Clients who seek out my services tend to be smart, self-aware, successful, spiritual, but struggling in relationship—A-G-A-I-N. You may identify as such a person. In my experience, the types of clients who find success share common features. See if any of these feel true for you:

- You're tired of the emotional rollercoaster and ready for real guidance from someone who's been there.
- You're stuck in patterns that keep your heart guarded — trapped between feeling you're "too much" and "not enough."
- You're unsure how to move forward—and need a practical step-by-step process that truly fits how you learn and grow.
- You're tired of carrying it all alone. You want a partner who's more than a lover—someone who truly has your back in life's ups and downs.
- You've spent years settling for crumbs—resentful, angry, and starving for the love you know is your birthright. Deep down, you're hungry for the full feast—and ready to claim it.
- You're a powerhouse at work—but can't understand why love feels like your blind spot.
- You secretly wonder if it's too late for you—and feel that sharp pang when you see couples who have what you long for.

Does this resonate with you?

Now, let me be clear: You haven't failed in love—you've simply outgrown old ways of relating. Now, you're ready to EMBODY a powerful, purpose-driven process that aligns with love you truly desire. This time, you're not just hoping—it's a wholehearted commitment. You're ready to do what it takes to make it real.

Welcome.

THIS IS AN INTERACTIVE EXPERIENCE

Let's be real: Information alone doesn't change lives. (You've read the books, so why hasn't this shifted yet?) It's the *implementation*—how you consistently use what you've learned to rewire your thoughts and behaviors—that creates real transformation.

That is why this book is designed to be interactive, filled with two powerful components to accelerate your growth:

The Love Lab Challenges: These are real-world practices and inquiries designed to take the insights from each chapter and ground them into your daily life. This starts the *unsexy* but necessary work of relational mastery. These challenges are your training ground, much like a martial arts dojo, where theory meets the action of transformation. They're meant to uncork your awareness. Stretch you. Stir up your resistance. And ultimately reveal your strength.

Creative Edge Experiences: You will find three guided creativity processes in this book. I hope they are fun, but they are also designed for function. They give your heart a way of metabolizing emotion, releasing old patterns, and reimagining your future through color, symbol, and image.

Why creativity? Because it's difficult to reach some parts of ourselves through language and words alone. Creativity opens doors that logic can't touch. It allows the subconscious to speak and the heart to come alive.

∾

Important note: Before you balk at these creative edge experiences, let me reassure you—you don't have to be "artistic" to do them. This is not about creating a product for others to see, criticize, and judge. They are not performative. This is also not about skill—it's about showing up to your process in a new, embodied way.

∾

Insights, awarenesses, and "ahas" will be revealed to you through your willingness to engage in them. Nothing changes until you are aware. So, here's the invitation: *Do the work.*

Even when it feels uncomfortable.

Especially then.

Your resistance is your personal *"You are here"* arrow. It shows you exactly where the growth wants to happen next.

This book isn't a bag of chips to mindlessly consume and toss aside—it's a slow, nourishing meal meant to be deeply digested, the memory of which will linger long after the last page.

Let yourself savor it.

You're smart enough to know results come from action. So, if you've been doing things the same way, expecting different results, this is your chance to interrupt the pattern.

If nothing else, use this book as an experiment in approaching things differently. A portal. A pathway. A new beginning.

Ready to begin?

Let's start with getting a finger on your relational pulse: In the resources section, you will find the link to a quiz that will help you discover where you are currently on your path to cultivating a deep, thriving relationship. Answer the questions as truthfully and honestly as possible; this will provide you with the most accurate sense of the work ahead for you.

When you have completed the test, come back to this point.

And let's get to work.

PART I
READYING THE SOIL

You have traveled too fast over false ground. Now your soul has come to take you back.

— JOHN O'DONOHUE

Before anything is planted, the soil must be prepared. In this section, we prepare your heart and mind—clearing out what no longer serves, softening the hard places, and enriching what's been neglected. The work you do here is invisible to others—tending to yourself with courage, honesty, and care.

LOVE: A WORKING DEFINITION

Our love was born outside the walls, in the wind, in the night, in the earth, and that's why the clay and the flower, the mud and the roots know your name.

— PABLO NERUDA

Love.

It's a word that carries untold meanings, shaped by upbringing, your past relationships, culture, and personal experiences. By the time you arrive here, reading this book, you already have a working definition for yourself—whether conscious or not—of what love is and what it isn't. That definition informs the way you move through relationships, how you receive and give love, and what you believe is possible when it comes to long-lasting, deep connection.

Now is the time to consciously recognize you've been operating under a definition that is not only incomplete but also built on an inherited understanding of love that was made for another time and place. What if the way you were taught to love was shaped by generational patterns, gender role norms, societal expectations, or even the survival strategies of those who came before you? What if the love you learned—while once necessary or protective—is incapable of helping you meet your intimacy needs as an adult?

To receive the most from this book, you and I need to work with the same foundation, a shared understanding. Because, if you have learned to see love as something transactional, as a currency you must earn, prove, or barter for, then the ideas introduced in this book will not land in the way they are meant to. But if you are willing to hold love in a new way, to consider that love is not something you *get* but something you *are inside of,* then the entire landscape of your relationships can change.

This is the definition of love that will guide us: **Love Is a Living System.**

Love is not something you earn. It's not a transaction, a bargaining chip, or a scarce resource to be handed out in exchange for good behavior. Love is not a tool to manipulate, control, or manage someone into behavior that is either acceptable or not overwhelming to you. When love is used as leverage—to keep people in line, to convince them into meeting your needs, or to withhold when they fail to meet your expectations—it ceases to be love. It becomes an act of coercion. A mechanism of control. A form of keeping score.

But love—the kind that withstands life's storms—is not a ledger or a scorecard. It's a circulatory system. When you embrace love as something that is always present, always moving, and always available, you step into a new way of relating with others. Love is there, even when things are hard, even when life and circumstances and stressors pull at the edges of your connection. It does not disappear in moments of tension or hardship. It doesn't need to be earned. It simply *exists.*

This way of loving asks you to take full responsibility for your inner world. It asks you to step out of the old, conditioned beliefs that have you smooshed between too much and not enough, that demand you to prove your worth, that tell you love is given only in exchange for something. With this love, you stand in the truth that you *belong,* that you are whole, and that you offer love freely without fear that it will run out.

And when you bring this understanding into your relationships with yourself and others—when love is no longer a negotiation but a steady, reciprocal flow—your connection becomes unbreakable. Love becomes an ecosystem, one that holds, sustains, and endures.

THERE ARE NO COINCIDENCES

Journeys end in lovers meeting.

— WILLIAM SHAKESPEARE

In the 1990s, I was handed a book called *The Celestine Prophecy* by James Redfield. It was a bit controversial at the time—even causing a heated disagreement with my ex, who was not remotely open to the ideas it contained. But the book opened my eyes to the possibility that life could be an intricate web of synchronicities guiding us toward deeper connection and growth. Every person we meet carries a message. Every encounter—big or small, joyful or playful—shapes our journey.

I found the concept intriguing.

Later, I was introduced to the legend of the Red Thread[1], which talks of an invisible cord connecting us to the people we are destined to meet. The thread is tied around our pinky finger and weaves its way through time, drawing us toward those who will play a significant role in our personal story. No matter how tangled, stretched, or strained it becomes, this thread never breaks.

Zen master Thich Nhat Hahn's concept of "Interbeing"[2] speaks to this same truth. He teaches that we do not exist as isolated individuals but as interconnected beings, deeply entwined with one another.

These teachings and many others invite us to see our relationships not as random encounters but as part of a greater design. Every connection, every heartbreak, and every moment of intimacy are stitches in the intricate tapestry of our lives. The Red Thread reminds us that love, growth, and transformation are always at play and in motion, guiding us toward deeper meaning.

They are also a reminder that no experience is wasted. No love is meaningless. Even the pain, even the endings—like in nature, where decay composts and creates the richest soil—everything has utility. Everything serves a purpose in our evolution.

This Red Thread legend is woven into the heart of my work. From it, the teachings of visionary artist and Intentional Creativity® founder Shiloh Sophia[3] and spiritual guide Don Miguel Ruíz[4], I've distilled five guiding principles.

1. **I Belong**. I am connected to you as you are to me. Because of this, I choose to be impeccable with my word and actions.
2. **I'm Responsible**. I tend to my part of the Red Thread as you tend to yours. Because of this, I do not take things personally.
3. **I Witness**. I see you as you see me. Because of this, I make no assumptions.
4. **I Choose**. I choose to be in this relationship with you. Because of this, I do my best, always.
5. **Love Guides Me.** In every moment, with every choice, love leads the way.

These five principles are not rules to measure yourself against or impossible ideals you must strive to uphold at all times. Instead, they are invitations—gentle reminders of the way home. We are, after all, human, messy, imperfect, and learning as we go. There will be moments when you forget this, when you act from fear instead of love, when you resist the thread rather than tend to it with care. This is the nature of being alive, of being in a relationship.

But the Red Thread remains constant.

The real work of being in relationship is not in being perfect, but in returning—over and again—to these principles, especially when relationships feel difficult, when you feel hurt, or you feel lost. These are the moments when remembering matters most. When choosing to lead with love, integrity, and responsibility has the power to shift everything.

Your evolution—our evolution, both as individuals and within this sacred web of connection—is woven through your willingness to do the real work. To keep showing up. To keep growing. To keep returning home to love.

THE COMMON DENOMINATOR

When we are no longer able to change a situation, we are challenged to change ourselves.

— VICTOR E. FRANKL

When I finally walked out of the psych ward, heart bruised but still beating, I had to rebuild my life from the ground up. Selling the home I'd shared and loved with my then-partner, deciding on a custody schedule with our dog, and moving into a new space were all part of the aftermath. As the dust settled, a bigger question emerged: I needed to do this love thing differently if I wanted it to work for me. But how?

One thing was perfectly clear: If I wanted a different outcome, I had to become a different version of myself.

Growing up, I didn't have a healthy model of love. But there was one couple—dear friends of my family—who did. We called them *Mamie and Pépère*, an elderly French couple whose love story was extraordinary. They had fallen in love as teenagers and had weathered decades, steadfastly devoted to one another, even through the trials of two world wars.

Their love wasn't about grand gestures or cinematic romance. It was about showing up. Day after day. Through joy and hardship. With tenderness and deep respect. Their partnership was a living testament of the Red Thread—what it means to choose someone, not just in the easy moments, but always.

Their example was a guiding light for me. They showed that love was possible.

And if it was possible, it was possible for me.

Their love stood in stark relief and contrast to all I had learned about relationships. It forced me to confront a hard truth.

The common denominator in all my failed relationships was **Me.**

In that moment of truth, I saw it clearly: I'd been carrying a deeply rooted belief about men—one shaped by my conditioning, my marriage, and the wreckage of my eight-year relationship. That belief had quietly governed every connection I'd formed, reinforced by wounds I had never tended to. And while I was not at cause for the pain that birthed it, the healing was mine to claim.

I was a proud card-carrying member of the *Men Are Pigs Club.*

In my world, secretly, I held the belief that men were assholes—unreliable, selfish, not to be trusted, incapable of deep love.

Except … that wasn't the full story.

Because *Pépère* wasn't an asshole. Neither were some of the other men I'd seen be kind, honorable, protective. Men who cherished their partners, even in conflict. Men who had their partner's back, no questions asked.

It'd just never been MY experience.

But, what if …?

What if men weren't inherently awful? What if the world was actually filled with mostly good men, men like *Pépère*? What if my beliefs were so off-center, I had been too blind to see their true nature?

That single *what if* cracked something open inside me. It inspired a yearlong experiment on men, a deep dive into understanding me—not through past hurts, but with fresh eyes.

But before I could start, I had to overcome the biggest internal hurdle of all.

SETTLING FOR CRUMBS

❦

Your desires are seeking you.

— MAMA GENA

At the time of all of these uncomfortable awarenesses, I was a first-year student at Mama Gena's School of Womanly Arts. There, I was searching for something: healing, sisterhood, and a new way forward after heartbreak. I didn't know it then, but I was about to come face-to-face with a truth I had been avoiding my entire life.

I was a single mother, exhausted, depleted, depressed, and desperate for change. I had spent years settling in love, saying yes to relationships that weren't a match, didn't serve me, accepting less than what I truly wanted, because deep down, I didn't believe I could actually have more.

It was during one of the experiential exercises led by Mama Gena herself that I had a profound awakening. She invited us to voice our deepest, wildest, most audacious desires—to name them, claim them, say them aloud. The room buzzed with excited energy as over 250 women unleashed their longing into the air. But me?

I went completely blank.

I couldn't think of a single thing I truly wanted. That realization plastered me into the chair: I had no idea how to desire. If I even dared venture into desiring, I was slapped down with *"But how? How am I going to make that happen? How could I have that? How could I even have it so good?"*

Growing up with Depression-era parents, I was taught that wanting more was selfish. "You get what you're given" was the adage I fed upon. Asking for anything extra—whether a second helping or special treatment—was met with derision, disdain, and a distinct dose of shame. Over time, I stopped asking altogether. I learned to settle, to take what was offered, to steal what was not.

To settle for crumbs.

That day in Mama Gena's classroom, I knew something had to change.

I reached out for support, and, as it turned out, I wasn't the only one struggling with accepting crumbs. A small circle of women and I banded together, determined to build our ability to want, to desire. We started small—co-creating a list of tiny desires, things as simple as a free cup of coffee, which grew into a desire for breakfast in bed—and grew bolder still. Soon, our list held visions of first-class weekends on tropical islands and Paris, candlelit dinners on a *bateau-moche* on the Seine, and everything in between.

The thing about desire that nobody talks about is this: You don't get to choose what you desire. Desire isn't logical. It doesn't follow rules. It isn't interested in what's convenient or appropriate. You don't get to reason your way into—or out of—what you deeply long for. In fact, desire often arrives uninvited, unsettling your carefully constructed plans, shining a light on parts of yourself you've diligently kept quiet.

You may choose not to act on your desire. You may suppress, numb, ignore, or shame it. But desire itself doesn't disappear. It's not compliant like that. It lives in your body, your bones, your belly. Left unattended, it doesn't become a quiet, obedient child. It finds workarounds—morphing into frustration, resentment, disconnection or even depression. But it's still there, beneath the surface, waiting to be heard.

So, the work isn't about controlling or erasing your desire. It's about being honest with yourself about *what* you actually want—and having the courage to speak it aloud, even if you may not be ready to act on it yet.

The list became my lifeline. It became my compass. And when I launched the Men Project, this list came with me.

~

The Love Lab Challenge: Ignite your Desire List. Your desire list isn't a to-do list; it's a permission slip to dream without limits. It's not about practicality or logistics; it's about fire, not function. As you write your list, notice when your mind tries to stop you with a "How." Don't let it. Your only job is to name what you want boldly, unapologetically. The "How" will take care of itself (as you'll see in the next chapter). Keep this list close and revisit it often. Add to it whenever the desire sparks. The more you connect with your desires, the easier it becomes to ask for and receive them. Trust that if you desire it, it is meant for you. And I stand for you getting exactly what you want.

THE MEN RESEARCH PROJECT

Have enough courage to trust love one more time and always one more time.

— MAYA ANGELOU

Recognizing my shortcomings—both in my ability to desire, and in the stories I had told myself about men made me know it was time for a change. If I truly wanted to be in a fulfilling relationship, I had to rewrite the story of love. I had to upgrade my Internal Operating System to meet my present need. I needed to:

- Know what I wanted;
- Ask for it;
- Allow men to show up and be of service; and
- Receive their attention, generosity, and kindness.

So, I set out on a bold experiment: to date as many men as I could for the singular purpose of changing my mind about them.

Loving me some science, I started with a hypothesis: *What if my*

beliefs about men are false, and the truth is that men are more like Pepère – kind,
generous, and trustworthy?

Like a good scientist, I created some parameters around the dates
themselves. Before agreeing to a date, I was upfront about my intentions. With each one of my prospects, I shared:

- I wasn't looking for a commitment.
- I felt ambivalent about men in general.
- I wanted to change my mind about them.
- Would they still be willing to go out on a date with me and
  help me?

This step alone sent many potential dates running for the hills. The
first point freed those seeking a commitment to finding someone else
aligned with their desires. The last three—an open request for support
and service—confused some, but intrigued others.

I mean, what kind of woman who gets on a dating app or is set up
with a blind date is so openly vulnerable and transparent from the
outset?

Men who had the capacity to handle that level of honesty, who said
"yes" to helping me, and "yes" to the date taught me my first lesson in
choosing a partner: Genuine honesty, sincerity, and transparency separate the wheat from the chaff.

After almost five decades of settling for chaff, I was finally
investing in wheat ....

I went into this project with two personal goals in mind:

1. To ask for what I wanted, unapologetically (I had my list,
   after all.) and
2. To ALWAYS leave the men I dated better than I found them.

Prior to my experiment, when a man asked, "What do you want to
do?" I'd freeze. I'd defer, shrink, and throw the question back at him.
"I don't know; what do you want to do?" Which always led to the

same forgettable, lackluster experience. No one ever left truly satisfied.

But now, I was ready.

I had spent time naming what lit me up, what excited me, and what brought me pleasure. So, when the question came, I could answer it with confidence. And in doing so, I gave my date a road map: a way to show up, plan something special, create a meaningful experience, and be the hero. My clarity guaranteed his success.

And all that was left for me to do?

Receive.

To let it in.

To revel in the attention, in the care, in the delight of having my desires met.

And here's something else: Because I consciously entered into this experiment with a scientific mindset, I felt I had nothing to lose. I set clear intentions, clear parameters, clear communication, and a clear outcome. That level of clarity made it easy to enter each date knowing one undeniable truth: I was already a catch.

They had no idea, but they were dating a Goddess.

And this changed *everything*.

That year, I dated all kinds of men: mechanics, lawyers, professors, business owners, construction workers, teachers, and more. Men with PhDs and men who were high school dropouts. Divorced men, life-long bachelors, and widowers still grieving the loss of the love of their lives. Some had children, others didn't. Some had traveled the world and spoke several languages; others had never left the region.

Before this experiment, I'd return home from a date and immediately start dissecting all the ways he hadn't shown up for me. How he hesitated when the check arrived, didn't hold the door, had an annoying habit, an offbeat sense of humor, or some other minor flaw (which I'd blow up into a major one). I'd pick him apart like a vulture over roadkill, searching for any reason to dismiss him, convinced he was just a disappointment, a pig, just like all the others.

But with my experiment underway, I deliberately flipped that habit on its head. And, instead of looking at all the reasons to disqualify a man, I made it my mission to track, document, and acknowledge all the ways he *was* a fit.

And in so doing, I made a profound discovery: No matter his background, income, education, profession, or life experience, every single man I dated possessed at least one quality I was looking for in a partner.

Each of them, in their own way, held a piece of the qualified partner puzzle.

They all had aspects of "the one."

Toward the end of that year, one man rose above the rest—a true *rara avis*, a rare bird to match my own uniqueness. There was something undeniably different about him, something that made me pause.

By that point, my heart had softened to every man. I had fully relinquished my lifetime membership to the *Men Are Pigs Club*. My mindset about men had shifted, my walls lowered, and, for the first time in a very long time, I was open—*truly open*—to the possibility of partnership.

What started as an experiment and an adventure became something more.

Over a decade later, we're still together. This legendary love affair is now my husband.

(And, for the record … he's still research. And he might note, still a catch!)

THINGS TO KEEP IN MIND

❦

Let no one enter who cannot see that the issues outside are a mirror of the issues inside.

— OTTO SCHARMER, *THEORY U*

Many of us carry the fantasy of a "perfect" relationship—a tall, ever-growing tree where everything feels effortless, harmonious, and perpetually blissful. This ideal, what I call the mythical "happily ever after," posits that love should be flawless. Love should be self-sustaining.

But here's the truth: There is no such thing.

Relationships are living, organic systems, not static states of perfection. They require watering, nurturing, pruning, and fertilizing through various seasons of growth. True relational success doesn't come from chasing perfection but from progressing through the four essential aspects of relational growth and sustainability: **Growing Down, Growing Up, Growing Together, and Flourishing.**

Amazingly, you don't even need to get to the end in order to experience peace, ease, joy, and connection. Growing Together can be plenty.

FOUR STAGES OF COMPETENCE

Learning does not follow a step one, two, three format. It's more of a cyclical, undulating, twisted about, messy process. Nothing about being human is tidy.

Let's put this on the table from the outset: You might be reading this because you're feeling at sixes and sevens yourself. You'll find that throughout this book, I'll offer several frames to keep in mind. These insights are intended to offer a broader perspective—a zoom-out view, if you will—to help you recognize two key truths: First, your messiness is not unique to you, and second, love fits a natural cycle.

Before we fully dive in, let's begin with two frameworks I have found particularly useful in helping clients to navigate change and relational growth. And change is what you're after!

The Four Stages of Competence[5] is the first framework. It is a learning model that describes the various psychological states we move through when learning a new skill. Its origins can be traced back to management coach Martin M. Broadwell, who developed the model in the 1960s to describe the different levels of learning. Originally, it portrayed four teachers who practiced at varying skill levels. It has since been adapted more broadly to apply to any competence.

Competence in this context can be defined as the ability to perform a task successfully. You're competent if what you want to do has the expected outcome or if whatever you produce actually works.

In relationships, competence shows up as emotional intelligence, discomfort resilience and relational skill. And, unlike the fairy tale notion of "happily ever after," the true point of being in relationship is not perfection; it's aliveness.

Choosing to be in relationship means embracing the full spectrum of your emotions, experiencing all eighty-eight keys of your emotional range. It's about playing these keys consciously, deliberately, and responsibly all in service of your relationship and personal growth.

~

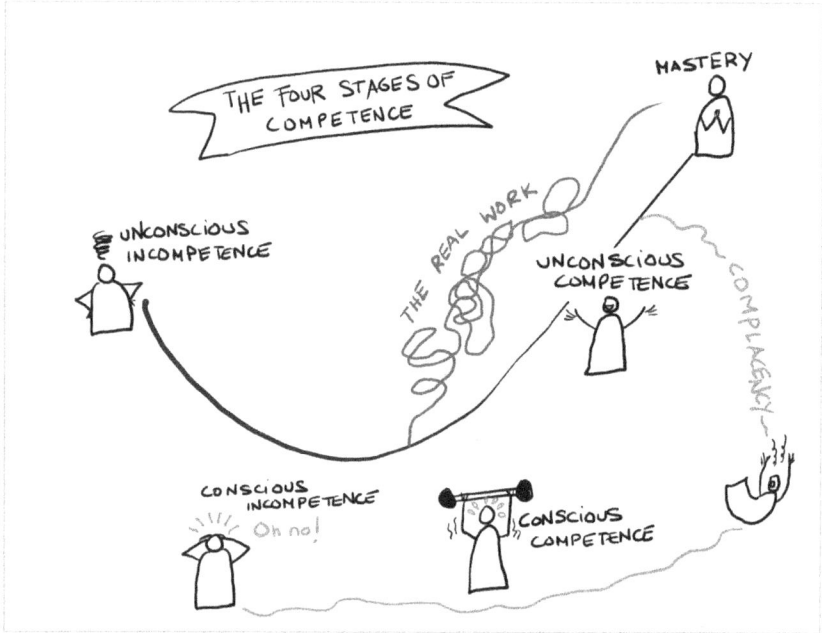

1. Unconscious Incompetence (Ignorance)

At this stage, you don't know what you don't know, and your lack of awareness is causing you to struggle. Whether due to ignorance, willful blindness, or naïveté, you may not even recognize that a particular skill is necessary. You likely take many mental shortcuts, remain unrealistically optimistic, and hold uninformed expectations. In this condition, you can't effectively help yourself or anyone else.

2. Conscious Incompetence (Awareness)

Here, you become aware of your ignorance. You recognize that what you don't know is a significant step in your relational growth. Although you still have no idea what you're doing, your analytical mind has kicked in, acknowledging your lack of skill. This awareness is what drives people to seek help—this is the stage where most clients reach out to me for support.

3. Conscious Competence (Practice)

You've learned something new. Now, you actually understand the "what" and the "why" of your actions. You can inquire, assess situations, and course correct based on practice and experience. While you function well at this stage, it requires forethought to stay on track as an ongoing and consistent practice—engaging in the heavy lifting work leading to mastery.

4. Unconscious Competence (Mastery)

You've practiced consistently, your skills are second nature. Your neural pathways have adapted, upgrading your Internal Operating System (IOS). In this stage, your relational actions feel effortless. You instinctively know how to navigate challenges without overthinking—it's simply a part of who you are.

~

Notice that at no stage of this competency model does it say someone else does the work *for* you. Growth and relational peace require personal responsibility at every step. This accountability is a non-negotiable ingredient in designing your relationship with intention.

The journey from unconscious incompetence (where you might currently find yourself) to unconscious competence needs two things:

- **Courage** to approach situations differently than you have in the past.
- **Commitment** to stay with the process through and beyond reaching a place of navigational certainty.

Are you in?

Love isn't a fairy tale—it's more like the growth of a tree. You can't expect a sturdy, flourishing relationship to thrive if you're building on shallow roots or expect instant results.

The number one reason people find themselves single or struggling in love? They're trying to grow a towering tree of love with the resources of a sapling. If you keep planting acorns of love but keep wondering why nothing's happening, it's not your worthiness in question—it's your relationship skills.

RELATIONSHIP GROWTH AND SUSTAINABILITY PHASES

Phase 1: Growing Down—Establishing Strong Roots

Key indicator: Unconscious incompetence.

In this phase, the foundation of your relationship is built. Like a tree establishing deep roots, this is where you learn to create trust, stability, and security. Often, you don't even know what you don't know at this stage. You must focus on developing an awareness of yourself and upgrading what I like to call your Internal Operating System (IOS).

Biggest Obstacle: Lack of awareness.

Your relationships often struggle because your own personal foundation isn't clearly established. You repeatedly experience the same kinds of heartbreak without understanding why.

Primary Goal: Develop deep roots of emotional resiliency.

Gather the tools you need for growth: coaching, support, and accountability. This is the time to stabilize your connection to yourself and learn what nourishes you personally in the long-term.

Phase 2: Growing Up—Reaching Skyward

Key Indicator: Conscious incompetence.

Now that your roots are firmer, you can grow upward and relate to others. Like a tree stretching toward sunlight, this is where you seek true connection from a more solid foundation. You are more aware of the things that have tripped you up relationally and are ready to try your budding skillset in the dating world.

Biggest Obstacle: Frustration and emotional resistance.

Practicing new skills when your old, familiar patterns keep getting activated is not for the faint of heart. When you're navigating unfamiliar territory and choosing to do things differently, it's easy to feel overwhelmed or inadvertently fall back into choosing mismatched partners. This is where frustration and emotional frustration arise—right at the edge of transformation.

Primary Goal: Strengthening emotional awareness and resiliency.

This phase is about tending to your roots while growing your skills with a potential partner. Learning patience and persistence as you face challenges. Understanding that growth takes time, attention, and consistent care.

Phase 3: Growing Together—Building Harmony

Key Indicator: Conscious competence.

Now, you and your partner have chosen to grow together. Like two trees with intertwined branches, you're learning to support one another interdependently while maintaining a sense of independence. At this stage, you're learning what feeds and nourishes your relationship. You know what needs to be done, and even though it may still require some thought, you're willing to continually upgrade your Relationship Operating System (ROS).

Biggest Obstacle: Overconfidence.

It's tempting at this juncture to think you've mastered the relationship game. Ongoing care is needed to keep Growing Together.

Primary Goal: Practice harmony in service of your Sacred Third Relationship (more on this later).

This is the phase where you both cultivate consistent practices —thoughtful communication, shared goals, and deepening trust. Your relationship thrives as you actively grow toward one another.

Phase 4: Flourishing—Full Bloom

Key Indicator: Unconscious competence.

Your relationship has fully flourished. Like a tree that's reached its full height, you're both standing tall, secure in your love and trust. You are truly a sanctuary for one another's hearts and a springboard to your mutual dreams. The skills and care you've developed have become second nature.

Biggest Obstacle (Yep, even here, you'll run across them.): Complacency.

Even a flourishing tree requires regular attention, nutrients, pruning, watering, and more to stay healthy and strong.

Primary Goal: Continue evolving (this is a lifetime practice).

Though your relationship is strong, staying open to change and growth as life shifts (guaranteed). Keep nurturing your connection to ensure your relationship continues to flourish. Especially in the face of new and reoccurring winds and storms life sends your way.

A RELATIONAL JOURNEY

In addition to the Four Stages of Competence, there's a second framework to keep in mind. That of transitional cues on your relational journey.

We are all heroes. Life is challenging. Living it fully—expressing the fullness of who you are in relationships—requires both the courage of a warrior and the softness, gentleness, and fluidity of a goddess.

In the 1940s, mythologist Joseph Campbell detailed the hero's journey in *The Hero with a Thousand Faces*, a road map for navigating life's challenges and fulfilling your calling. This framework acknowledges the fear and risk inherent in embarking on transformative paths, much like relationships. The hero's journey is an ancient structure that guides you through life's greatest challenges toward your deepest gift as a human being. While everyone's journey is unique, the well-traveled paths of the heroes that came before offer wisdom and direction. Campbell's hero's journey aligns with a more masculine paradigm.

Depth psychologist Anne Davin[6] reimagined the framework as the Heroine's Journey. Through a feminine lens, she offers a different perspective on personal fulfillment, romantic love, and visionary leadership. Grounded in her clinical experiences as a mental health professional and informed by indigenous practices, her model addresses the very real social conditions and oppression that exist for women.

Beneath the surface of every woman—the version the world sees—lives someone greater: one seeking a true reflection of oneself beyond negative cultural stereotypes and outdated models of masculine power and success.

These are the models I use with my clients to support and honor natural cycles of relationships and life. This approach supports you in accessing your highest impact, power, and purpose.

TRANSITIONAL CUES IN YOUR JOURNEY

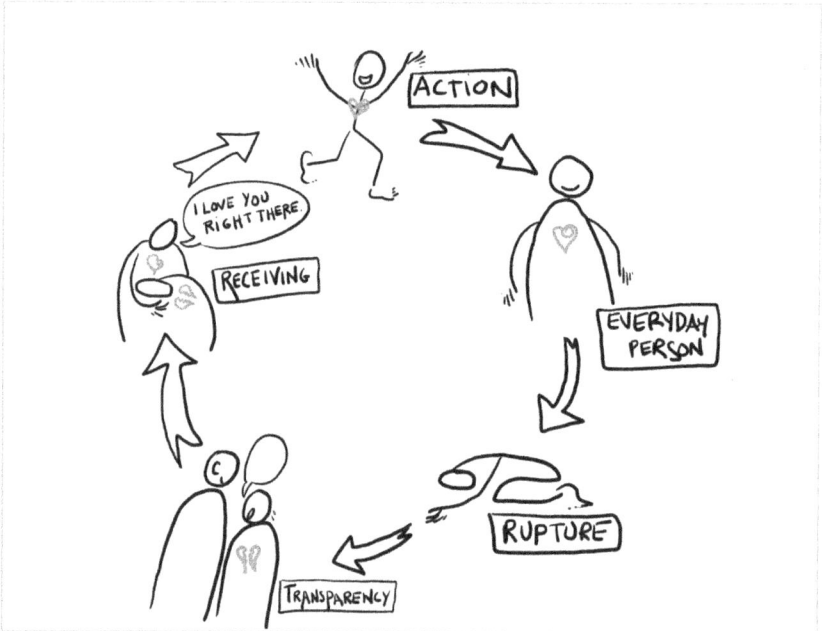

As you move through the phases of Relationship Growth and Sustainability, certain indicators denote moments of transition. These moments occur at intervals throughout your life, each bring their own intensity and wisdom, each is marked by specific cues. Together, they form a sacred spiral of growth, one that invites you to embody your full essence with courage and grace.

EVERYDAY EXPERIENCE

Your journey might begin here, as the modern everyday individual—someone like you, consciously living your life and embracing self-care as a spiritual practice. This is a moment that nurtures self-awareness, setting the foundation for deeper transformation. But life's about to shift. A rupture is coming, a spark ignited by your inner genius to evolve your connection to the divine.

RUPTURE

This moment is marked by an activating event that shakes your world. It could be the loss of a loved one, a breakup or divorce, a career shift, or a move. Rupture creates the perception of loss, forcing you to see yourself and your life in an entirely new way. Here this question arises: "Who am I now?" The spiritual practice in this phase is surrender—letting go of control and trusting the unfolding process.

TRANSPARENCY

Stepping into the transformative power of vulnerability is a key element of this moment. Transparency invites you to fully embrace your emotional intensity and the multifaceted aspects of your self. Rather than resisting the chaos within, you come to see it as essential —beautiful, nourishing, and vital for your growth. The spiritual practice here is to become a vulnerable observer: Valuing your emotional experiences, witnessing them with compassion, and understanding that this observation is your greatest source of strength and protection.

RECEIVING

As you move into the next moment, you soften further. Receiving asks you to remain open, exposed, and vulnerable while allowing others to tend to you. This stage teaches the sacredness of being nurtured and cared for, reminding you that your strength lies in accepting support during times of crisis. The spiritual practice is compassionate receptivity—welcoming love and care as an act of self-honor.

ACTION INTO RAPTURE

Here, you are guided into action leading to rapture. This moment is marked with profound emotional and spiritual restoration, where you emerge with new attitudes, perspectives, revitalized energy, and a deep sense of purpose. Your grit and grace from the previous stages transform into sacred service, creating a life that feels aligned, meaningful, and deeply connected. The spiritual principle is sacred service —offering your hard-earned wisdom and grace to the world.

These moments are not a linear path; they follow a cyclical rhythm of life, repeating with each new season of change. As you honor these moments as the natural way of things, you'll come to see them not as disruptions but as gifts—each one carrying you closer to the most radiant, authentic expression of your divine essence.

These indicators of transition call you to release the belief that you are a victim of a cruel, random act by a hostile universe. Embracing this perspective is a revolutionary shift—a transformation from victim to hero and heroine. It's a recognition that something far greater than your immediate circumstances is unfolding, guiding you toward profound growth and purpose.

READYING THE SOIL

Before a tree ever stretches skyward, it first sends its roots deep into the earth. So, too, with love.

All that you have read so far—reframing love as a circulatory system, honoring synchronicity and sacred connection through the Red Thread, the radical self-honesty of recognizing your own patterns, and the deep excavation of your desires—has been in service of one sacred task: **preparing the ground.**

You are not broken. But you have been taught to love in ways that don't support your wholeness. With this first section laying bare those teaching—not to judge or shame them, but to instead witness them clearly. Only by seeing what you've inherited can you begin to choose something new.

Your relational foundation matters.

In nature, a tree that grows too fast, whose roots remain shallow will topple at the first storm. The same is true for relationships. The deepest, most connected partnerships are not those without conflict or challenge—they are the ones built on inner rootedness, conscious choice and emotional resiliency.

In truth, you cannot *grow with* another until you've learned to *grow down* into yourself.

In the next section, we enter **Growing Down**, the essential inner work of unearthing the unconscious patterns, beliefs, and inherited systems that quietly run in the background of your relationship life. This is where you strengthen your emotional roots, build internal stability, and upgrade your Internal Operating System. This is the sacred descent that must precede the rise.

It may not be glamorous, but if you are willing to do the work, it is transformational.

The deeper your roots, the taller your tree.

And this is where your real love story begins.

PART II
GROWING DOWN

To be rooted is perhaps the most important and least recognized need of the human soul.

— SIMONE WEIL

Relationships are not built on surface changes. They are first built inside you, by digging deep. Growing Down is your opportunity to uncover old patterns, outdated beliefs, and survival strategies that shaped your past. It gives you the chance to update them to meet your present relational needs. By Growing Down, you lay the groundwork for a love within that can weather all storms.

THE WATER YOU'RE
SWIMMING IN

And in that moment of recognition, this is when we save ourselves, from the self that was never real to begin with. This is when we see with the eye of the heart.

— MEGGAN WATTERSON

If you're holding this book, chances are you're a high achiever—a powerhouse in your chosen field, deeply capable, profoundly gifted, one who has spent a lifetime building the skills and strategies that got you there. You've worked hard, honed your expertise, and built a sense of success that many admire. But let's be real: Success likely came at a cost. To thrive in your professional world, you may have had to armor up, adopting a tough exterior to navigate challenges and setbacks. Armor protects, but may have also built a wall around your heart.

Here's the rub: The very skill set that propelled you forward in your career could be the very barrier that is blocking love. You might have approached love with the same strategic mindset, only to feel stuck in a frustrating pattern, asking yourself:

- Why do I keep attracting people who only want a one-night stand?
- Why do my relationships start off hot and then fizzle out?
- Why can't anyone meet me in my power *and* pain?
- Why are they intimidated by my achievements?"
- Why do I feel smooshed between too much and not enough?

Do any of these questions resonate? If so, you're not alone. These questions don't make you broken; they make you human.

You might carry a spiritual depth that doesn't get airtime—a part of you you've kept under wraps to appear professional, polished, and credible to be taken seriously. But in doing so, you've also tucked away a vital piece of yourself: your creative fire, your sensual pulse, the playful, intuitive, joy-seeking self you once trusted. That part of you didn't vanish—it just got quiet. And maybe, just maybe, you're tired of being the strong one. Tired of holding it all together. Tired of carrying the weight of the world while wondering if anyone ever will carry you—or simply walk beside you to hold some of what you've been holding alone.

You want to feel safe enough—both on your own *and* with a partner—to fully express your true nature, all while holding onto every ounce of your hard-earned success.

Deep down, you know that on the other side of this stuckness is the kind of legendary love you were always meant for.

In truth, the things that make your professionally successful can quietly sabotage your intimate relationships. When you don't feel truly safe or fully seen, you default to presenting the polished, socially acceptable version of yourself—the one that performs, impresses and protects. But behind that mask, the more vital parts of you go unmet. And so you attract mismatched partners—people who connect to the version of you you've curated, not the totality of who you are. What works in the boardroom becomes a barrier in the bedroom. Those same traits that help you lead, solve, and deliver can keep you from the intimacy, vulnerability, and depth your heart truly longs for.

Fragmented, you are present as one person "out there" and another in your PJs at home.

If your success is built by toughening up and erecting walls around yourself, it can lead to more pain. Unknowingly, you may be creating the very situations you're trying to protect yourself from, ultimately attracting what you fear most. The effort of putting on the armor, to present, posture, and go to battle each day is absolutely exhausting. This fragmentation leads to quiet suffering in shame, anger, and depression.

I can say this with confidence because I spent decades living behind armor.

Honestly, you need not get more haggard or grow wearier as the years go by. You need to *stop fighting who you really are*—and begin aligning the way you operate with what you actually need now.

To make those necessary shifts, it's essential to adopt a mindset of curiosity and adventure, developing a Love Lab of sorts—a place to explore and conduct research on your Internal Operating System (IOS). Your IOS are the strategies, coping mechanisms, default patterns, and beliefs that unconsciously shape how you navigate the unique landscape of your world.

To begin this first phase of your relational process, Growing Down, you must courageously dig down into your roots, become conscious of your current IOS, and begin the real work of upgrading it to meet your needs as an adult. This ensures the tree that grows from those roots (a.k.a. YOU) is viable, healthy, resilient, and capable of weathering relationship storms, anchored in clarity, calm, and confidence. When we work with your unique nature, growth becomes inevitable.

I once heard about a cartoon that captured this idea perfectly: two fish above the water, one who is completely unaware of the water itself until the other points it out. It's a simple but powerful image for what happens when we are made aware of the hidden influences that shape us—family, culture, institutions. We don't even realize we're floundering until someone or something helps us see the water we've been swimming in all along.

We all have blind spots. Our willingness to see them is the beginning of change.

YOUR INTERNAL OPERATING SYSTEM (IOS): ROOT INTO CLARITY

❦

Under duress, we don't rise to our expectations, we fall to our level of practice.

— BRUCE LEE

Awareness precedes change. Change can only begin when we acknowledge our current state. When operating on autopilot, guided by outdated routines, habits, beliefs, and behavior patterns coded by past rather than present needs, we are kept in an eternal loop of suffering. Awareness forces you to pause and take a closer look.

Awareness isn't just about what you do; it's about *why* you do it.

Behind every habit, there's a motive, a belief, or an emotional trigger. For change to occur, you must uncover the underlying factors that have created your current experience. Although awareness may be the key to relational change, it is not enough alone. What's needed is the real work of Growing Down.

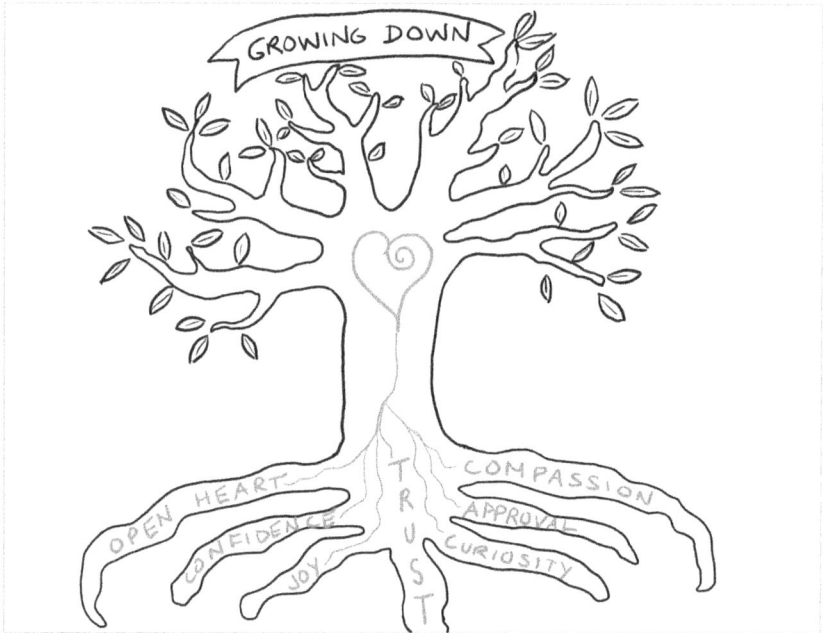

Another way to look at growth and maturity is to not look exclusively at reaching upward in skills and power but rather to also look at the depth of your roots. True development mirrors nature, just as the tallest trees extend their roots downward even as they stretch toward the light.

That is, we grow not only upward—not only skyward—but down into the earth. By doing so consistently, in time, you become more rooted and resilient, more capable of surviving storms, and less shaken away from yourself or others by idle wind or rain. Growing Down is putting awareness into action. It is about consciously doing the real work—which is not for the faint of heart. It means being willing to:

- Overcome resistance to self-examination. Looking inward can be uncomfortable, but it's a crucial step to the process.
- Illuminate blind spots. These can be uncovered through introspection, feedback, and the guidance of a coach or mentor.

- Activate patience and persistence. Trust in the process.
- Tame your fear of change that keeps you from looking too closely, maintaining the illusion of comfort and security.
- Courageously examine denials that prevent you from facing uncomfortable truths.

By becoming more aware of how you've been operating in your relationships and choosing to respond differently, you begin taking responsibility for your part. In other words, you are taking ownership of your piece of the Red Thread.

You must be willing to do what it takes to uncover and upgrade your IOS—those patterns quietly running beneath the surface. First comes awareness. Then clarity. And finally, the discipline to turn that awareness and clarity into consistent, aligned action—action that honors who you are becoming and supports your current relational needs. Over time, you retrain yourself into a new way of relating that feels much less effortful.

Let me be clear: I am far from finished with my own work. I'm not speaking to you from a childhood steeped with encouragement, acceptance, or unconditional love. I wasn't taught to trust myself - my intuition, my creative nature, or my intelligence. I didn't grow up without fears for my physical safety or emotional well-being. My parents carried their own trauma and addiction. And I didn't live out a fairy tale of happy, abuse-free marriage or tidy ever after relationships.

My story was one of survival.

None of this is to say that your story mirrors mine. Each of us has our own past. The key to my experience—what I bring to you as a coach—is that my journey toward love forced me to develop tools capable of overcoming those challenges.

I was sent away at sixteen years of age for not following the accepted rules and for bringing attention to my family's inherent dysfunction, abuse, and addiction with my adolescent, rebellious behavior. This was unacceptable to my father, who, as a civil servant for the United Nations, accustomed to dealing with movers and shakers, ambassadors, and the like, felt threatened that my behavior would destroy his reputation.

As I'm sure you can imagine, being banished and sent across the ocean was a defining moment in my life. I went from having the experience of relying on my understanding of what a family was, living with my parents and siblings, to suddenly having my world turned upside down, living with an aunt I barely knew in a country I didn't understand.

What I've come to understand is that I carried this past experience into all of my relationships. It left me with a sense of desperation and a belief that I was disposable. I longed for someone to love me, catch me, provide for me, hold me. I didn't see it at the time—but years later, it became painfully clear. That awareness surfaced when I lost myself completely in shame, hustling to prove my worth while feeling anything but.

In 2008, the same year the stock market crashed, I hit rock bottom. I lost my boyfriend, my blended family, my home, my dog, and quit my then twenty-year teaching job without a Plan B and no savings to speak of.

I went into that very, very dark place. The depth of the depression, discouragement, disenfranchisement, hopelessness, shame, embarrassment, anger, and grief I felt then was almost beyond description.

As I slowly made my way back to life, one thing became painfully clear: I couldn't live like that anymore. Anaïs Nin's quote—*"And the day came when the risk to remain tight in a bud was more painful than the risk it took to blossom."*—became both a mantra and a lifeline. I was done living in shame, no longer willing to hide or stifle myself.

I was done with twisting myself into pretzels to be more acceptable. I was done with saving my anger and resentment for the moments I'd had enough wine to say what needed saying. Done burning down people's villages, instead of learning to speak up. Done compromising, lying, disapproving of myself. Done feeling disenfranchised. All. The. Time.

It was time to risk the discomfort of blossoming.

The shame, anger, depression, and the endless hustling for worth took me down a deep dark path. And, had I known what I am about to share with you now, I believe my experience could have been vastly different. My story is uniquely mine, as is yours. Yet I'm confident that threads of my story run through yours—even if the details are distinctly different.

~

The Love Lab Challenge: What are your unique Internal Operating Instructions—the unconscious rules that drive how you show up in relationships?

Give yourself full permission to be shamelessly honest. Your task is to uncover the core beliefs and stories you already live by—the ones that govern your moment-by-moment choices, emotions, and reactions in real time. Then, name them clearly and consciously.

I've provided some examples to get you started:

- I must be needed to be loved.
- I can't trust anyone fully.
- Unless I'm productive (doing), I'm worthless.

Now it's your turn. What silent rules are running the show?

Growing Down means becoming aware of these old patterns. This is not about blame. It's about responsibility—the empowered, holy kind.

DISCOMFORT RESILIENCE: REWRITE YOUR STORY

> *We don't see things as they are, we see things as we are.*
>
> — ANAÏS NIN

Let's talk about discomfort. Specifically, cultivating resilience.

Oftentimes, what we do with partners is to use them as our emotional anchor—the person you go to feel safe and soothed. When you were little, you had a guardian, and they were the place you went to whenever you were spooked, or scared, or confused. Whether you received support or not, that person became your source of safety. It's coded in your mind that this figure is the place to go for rescuing when the world is overwhelming. As a young child, you're not born with the ability to regulate your nervous system to calm yourself. No child knows how to self-soothe, so they depend on the caretaker's system, usually their mother, because mothers are entrained (or synced) with theirs. When the mother finds a state of calm, so can the child.

Parents—being human—are imperfect in countless ways. As a parent myself, I know this to be painfully true. And, to whatever degree our parents were able to manage their own dysregulation and discomfort—that's the degree we learned to regulate ours. As children, we didn't just listen to words—we felt our caregiver's nervous systems. When they could stay steady, we could start to feel safe. That tracking—of their steadiness, their presence—is how we first learned what calm feels like. It's where regulation begins.

But if that wasn't available to you—or only inconsistently—you may now find yourself trying to do this, unmodeled, alone.

So the question becomes: How do you offer this to yourself now, as an adult?

According to the psychological and spiritual teachings of *A Course in Miracles*, the ego, the voice of fear, thrives in confusion[7]. That might sound surprising. But think about it: When you're confused, anxiety and fear naturally follow. You loop. You spin. You stall. The confusion keeps you circling familiar ground, making it harder to move forward. And without movement, there's stagnation—a slow drift from yourself, from others, from the wisdom that lies within you.

Call it intuition, Spirit, Universe, God, or Source, it matters not. What matters is that confusion severs connection. And connection is the very thing we're wired for.

Being connected to yourself and your inner wisdom opens the door to growth, expansion, and more genuine relationships. When you're disconnected—which manifests as anxiety, fear, doubt, worry, or panic—relationships suffer. Confusion makes it hard to feel confident or secure in your connections. If you desire deep relational expression, you need less effort, and more flow, not friction.

Without managing your discomfort, the chatter of your monkey mind takes over. And takes you out of the present and into survival mode—spinning stories, catastrophizing outcomes, and replaying old scripts. When your thoughts start to race, it's easy to fall back into familiar ways of coping. You might throw yourself into overwork, lose yourself in caring for everyone else, or slip into the numbing comforts of food, alcohol, social media scrolling, or binge-watching programs. These distractions offer short-term relief, but they come at a long-term cost: disconnection from yourself, your body, your truth, your needs. They create just enough static to drown out the call from within—the one asking for your attention, your tenderness, and your care.

A friend once described numbing like being in the driver's seat of a car, speeding down the highway at eighty miles per hour, fast asleep at the wheel. Disconnection follows. And with disconnection comes loneliness, which leads back to confusion, opening the floodgates to endless questioning:

- What do I do next?
- What am I doing wrong?
- Who am I being?
- Is who I'm being enough?
- Will people love me for me?
- Will I ever find the kind of love I want?
- Are my standards too high?
- Am I asking too much?

These questions keep your mind spiraling—NOT the space from which healthy relationships emerge. Your role, if you hope to change, is to learn to regulate your nervous system. To manage the discomfort brought by doubt and confusion. These feelings are natural. Your practice is to discover how they are activated by limiting beliefs or outdated narratives and to understand that they can be shifted. Managing discomfort means creating a steady container for your emotional state—one that helps you shift from confusion, doubt, anxiety, and fear into greater certainty, safety, and trust.

Resilience to discomfort is an act of responsibility as well as a moment-by-moment choice to remain connected, no matter what. It is the willingness to do what it takes to retrain your nervous system to feel safe when you are connected not remain addicted to confusion you have grown accustomed to. It's a practice you must dedicate yourself to each and every day.

Now before you poo-poo me around this idea, remember you are not looking for short-term relief but for a different way of being. A new normal. This being the case, consider discomfort management nonnegotiable—this IS what it takes to redress yourself when you've been hijacked by your ego, or fear-based mind. Whether you accept it or not, you are in a retraining process.

There are several ways to manage your discomfort and disconnection. For example, breathing practices, movement, meditation, journaling, exercising, aromatherapy, baths, rituals, and self-pleasure, to name a few. You can connect with a friend, read an inspiring book, or say a prayer. You name it. All of these are wonderful practices. I highly recommend that you dial up your daily dose.

What we are interested in here, is in interrupting old patterns in real time, and creating tangible, trackable, ongoing evidence of new ways of operating. This is so you don't find yourself believing nothing has really changed or be easily influenced to give up on yourself (especially when you're around others), and self-sabotaging. This is why you commit to practices, this process, and consistently honoring your pace, no matter what.

It's what I refer to as doing the "real relational work" of developing conscious competence. Here you take what you've learned about yourself, your beliefs, the stories you've told yourself, and practice course corrections. These may be small and subtle. At other times, life-changing. It is how you choose moment to moment, every day, to move from rupture, to action, to rapture. To be the hero or heroine of your own relational journey.

And ... you won't want to do it.

Your unhelpful habit cycles—the ones that pull you off course from what you truly care about—have a sneaky way of showing up when you least expect them. They'll snap you back into old patterns that sabotage your intentions and derail you desire for change. Why? To avoid the discomfort that comes with growth. These patterns distract, numb, or try to control your inner experience, pulling you away from the values you're working so hard to live into.

The Snap-Back Effect, a term coined by Dr. Maxwell Maltz, author of *Psycho-Cybernetics*[8], describes what happens when we unconsciously sabotage our efforts to grow or change. Think of a rubber band: It can only be stretched so far for so long before it snaps back to its original shape. The same thing happens with our habits. You start strong, but eventually, you get tired, discouraged, bored, or distracted. You lose focus. And without even realizing it, you slide back into old behaviors and default patterns—the familiar identity you've always believed was just who you are.

This is where being responsible for your piece of the Red Thread comes in.

Yes, it is human to snap back. Yes, you'll resist the change. Yes, you'll want to give up, cry "Uncle," and beat the drum of "this doesn't work for me."

I get it.

But through consistent, daily practices, you will see yourself solidly transforming over time. You will look back to where you've come from and recognize you are not behaving, thinking, or believing the same old stories. Your mind becomes clear, expanded. Your heart clearer, expanded. Your soul, clear and expanded. You're free.

Does that not feel better?

∽

The Love Lab Challenge: When you begin to disrupt old relational patterns, discomfort will arise. Confusion. Doubt. Fear. Temptation to shut down, numb out, or lash out. A discomfort resilience tool I recommend starting with is pattern interrupt and breath reset. The preliminary work is intended to increase your awareness of your current IOS functioning.

Preliminary work

Remember: Think about times you've been dysregulated. Become aware of what happened in those moments by taking the time to put pen to paper and reflect on the following:

- What do I physically reach for?
- How do I feel or react emotionally?
- What habits relating to how I interact with others are warning signals that I am headed into distress?
- What habits do I engage in feel good in the moment, but have a negative impact the next day or long-term?

In Real-Time

- Catch the pattern. Notice the warning signals that you're moving into a dysregulated state.
- Pause. LITERALLY, stop what you're doing.
- Breathe. Take five long, slow breaths.
- Name what's happening. "I'm feeling [emotion—e.g., anxious] right now."
- Choose one small action to connect you to certainty, safety, and trust.

Commit to this practice for the next seven days. And then, if you're willing, for a month more. Track it. Notice what shifts. I guarantee things will.

This is how you create a new relational muscle: becoming someone who can hold tension, stress, and love without collapsing, armoring up, or abandoning yourself.

Regulating your inner world, though, is only half the equation. The next is how you protect and express that truth in relationship through establishing aligned boundaries.

VALUES AND BOUNDARIES

Your task is not to seek for love, but merely to seek and find all the barriers within yourself that you have built against it.

— RUMI

Once you've begun anchoring yourself and understanding your inner world, through the awareness of your nervous system and emotional regulation, the next step in learning is to define—and most importantly, honor—your edges.

Edges are where personal boundaries come to play. Not as hard walls but as the living, breathing spaces where your values, needs, and truth exist. They shape who and how you love, lead, and allow yourself to be loved in return.

BOUNDARIES

Having boundaries means clarity about the ways you've let things slide—when you say *yes* but mean *no*, when you compromise too quickly, when you let yourself and others off the hook. Each time you do, you chip away at your relationship with yourself. And when that happens, it shows up everywhere: in how you and others treat your time, money, energy, and worth. This is where many get stuck. They believe the issue they are experiencing is related to time, money, or how they are being disrespected. But those are just symptoms.

The root cause? A lack of connection to your own sense of worth. Instead of taking personal responsibility by shoring up your sense of entitlement—the rightful kind—or standing in your innate value, you seek answers outside of yourself. In truth, the real shift begins inside —in your willingness to Grow yourself Down by claiming your right to courageously ask for what you need, take up space, and honor what matters most to you without apology.

Let's begin there.

The Love Lab Challenge: Before continuing to read, take a moment to check in with yourself. What does the word "boundary" mean to you? You may have an actual definition or have examples of how you or others create or establish boundaries with yourself and/or with others. Don't skip this step. It's always good to know where you are located on any map as a frame of reference before continuing your journey.

Now that you've a baseline of what boundaries mean to you, let's start with one I will use as a working definition. Let's first clarify what boundaries are *not*:

- They aren't a tool for self-punishment, guilt, or anxiety.
- They aren't about restricting others.
- They aren't the same for everyone.
- They don't make you unhappy.
- They don't limit your joy.

- They aren't rigid or unchangeable.
- They aren't about being right or wrong.

The *Oxford English Dictionary* defines a boundary as "a line that marks the limits of an area, a dividing line." In relationship, personal boundaries are less about controlling others and more about how you respond to their trespasses. Instead of expecting others to adjust their behavior to meet your needs, a personal boundary means you claim responsibility for how you'll show up, what you'll allow, and what you'll do to honor your well-being if a line is crossed.

When it comes to relationship boundaries, it's easiest to think of them as clear and respectful communication. They let others know what you're comfortable or uncomfortable with in relationship. They clarify your physical and emotional limits. The beliefs you hold true.

Melody Beattie[9], in *Beyond Codependency,* wrote, "Setting boundaries is about learning to take care of ourselves, no matter what happens, where we go, or who we're with."

In essence:

- Boundaries arise from clear decisions about what we do and don't deserve.
- They stem from the belief that we, our desires, likes, and dislikes matter.
- They reflect a deeper understanding of our personal rights, especially the right to care for and be ourselves.
- Boundaries are built as we learn to value, trust, and listen to ourselves and our connection to Spirit.
- They allow us to be both separate and connected.

Boundaries serve as the rules we set for ourselves within relationships, starting with the relationship with ourselves. While they can be fluid depending on social setting or cultural context, some boundaries are absolute, like those involving sexual consent, where zero tolerance for abuse is nonnegotiable. The absolute boundaries, or *deal-breakers,* help us act swiftly and decisively when they're crossed. Other boundaries, however, can be more challenging to clarify.

Personal boundaries are not always visible; they are psychological and shaped by experience. There are three main types of personal boundaries: thin, thick, and graceful.[10] Most people have a mix but may lean toward one particular type depending on the situation.

Thin Boundaries

Thin boundaries are often learned as a defense in childhood when a person wasn't allowed to develop healthy personal limits. A child who wasn't allowed privacy, autonomy, or the right to protest may grow up with blurred boundaries. As an adult, they may overshare, struggle to say "no," become overinvolved in others' problems, and rely heavily on others' opinions, often accepting disrespect or abuse to avoid rejection.

Thick Boundaries

Thick boundaries, on the other hand, are built to protect from either physical or emotional pain. Socially, thick boundaries may present as an avoidant attachment style or as defenses, such as blaming others, to shield oneself from shame. A person with thick boundaries may avoid intimacy, rarely ask for help, and maintain few close relationships. They guard personal information and keep others at a distance to avoid the risk of being hurt or rejected.

Graceful Boundaries

Graceful boundaries lie somewhere in between. Picture the way a well-tended garden gate functions: sometimes wide open to welcome visitors, sometimes partially closed to maintain privacy, and sometimes firmly shut to signal a need for solitude. Similarly, a person with clear boundaries knows when to open up and when to close off. They are self-aware, understand their own values, and share information appropriately. They communicate their needs and accept when others say "no" without resentment.

Boundaries, in this sense, aren't just lines; they are dynamic and adaptable, allowing us to navigate relationships with both strength and grace.

However, we have been shaped by parents who had different opportunities than we do. We forget that the cultural habits we were raised with belong to generations that lived in different realities. As a result, we cannot update these habits quickly enough. No matter where you find yourself in your evolution, you are bumping up against a whole series of invisible "no's" that aren't necessarily yours. No's you inherited that you can begin to play with and to rework. These internal "no's" —the ones that keep you from moving forward—are very much like the plastic owls found in Amtrak station parking lots. They're placed there to scare pigeons and mice. And it works, not because the owls are real, but because to the pigeons and mice, they look like danger. They signal, *watch out, don't go there, it's not safe.* Our limiting beliefs function the same way. They seem convincing. They look like the truth. But when we don't pause to question, we repeat familiar, unhelpful patterns, scared off by something that wasn't real to begin with.

We also have a fascinating relationship with the word "no." It is a boundary-setting word deeply tied to desire—what we want, what we stand for, and what we're willing to allow. Troubles arise when asking for what we want means risking a "no," whether giving or receiving it. And that risk can stir up unpleasant and uncomfortable feelings— rejection, shame, the fear of not being safe or accepted.

Then there's the internal "no," that invisible one. It lives in the stories we tell ourselves, in the protective mechanisms we've put into place that keep us from showing up fully or asking for more. And when we don't say "no" when it's needed, we end up shrinking, compromising, and putting our needs last. It's like wearing a jacket that's two sizes too small, tight, uncomfortable, unsustainable. Eventually, that kind of self-abandonment has consequences:

- Unfulfilling relationships emerge, where saying "yes" comes at the cost of personal truth, leading to resentment or feelings of being manipulated.
- Anxiety arises from a disconnection between one's desires, goals, and your inner guidance—fragmenting access to intuitive intelligence.
- Prioritizing others over desires may become a of self-protection, but often leads to stress, depletion, and a diminished ability to give from a resourced and nourished place.
- Over time, this creates a loop—a recurring cycle of relational dissatisfaction, anxiety, and stress that ultimately spirals to shame. And shame, once activated, tends to

perpetuate like a snake eating its own tail: difficult to interrupt and hard to escape.

VALUES

Setting boundaries begins with knowing what you stand for. That means having clarity on your desires, values, what you will and will not tolerate, and your deal-breakers. Boundaries are not just protection—they're about aligning your beliefs and actions. As Alexander Hamilton purportedly said, "If you don't stand for something, you'll fall for anything." This is where the real work begins.

Your personal core values reveal what you stand for. When you know what you stand for, you open to only what aligns with your deepest-held truths. From this clarity, your boundaries can be clearly defined and more easily expressed.

~

The Love Lab Challenge: Use your values to create personal boundaries aligned with who you are at your core. These boundaries adapt appropriately to your surroundings and are powerful:

1. Begin by identifying your top ten core values from the list below. It is not a comprehensive list, but rather a jump start. Use what you choose, and add your own, as needed.
2. From that list, whittle it down to your top five values.
3. And finally, select your top three values.

Abundance	Achievement	Adventure	Authority
Beauty	Being of Service	Change	Commitment
Communication	Compassion	Competition	Cooperation
Courage	Creativity	Decisiveness	Discipline
Effectiveness	Excellence	Fairness	Family
Financial Well Being	Freedom	Fun	Generosity
Good Health	Happiness	Harmony	Honesty
Humor	Independence	Integrity	Knowledge
Love	Loyalty	Peace	Personal Growth
Perfection	Power	Punctuality	Relationships
Religion / Spirituality	Resourcefulness	Safety	Simplicity
Sobriety	Stability	Status	Success
Tolerance	Tradition	Trust	Truth

∼

Your values can be used to create personal boundaries that align with who you are at your core. As such, they are extremely powerful. For each of your core values, you want to identify the following:

- What will you <u>allow</u> in your space, your life, and your relationships, given this value?
- What will you <u>tolerate</u> in your space, your life, and your relationships (but don't like) given this value?

- What <u>won't you allow</u> in your space, your life, your relationships, and business given this value?

Example: Let's say, integrity is a top value for you. What you might better understand through the above questions might look like:

- You allow those who are genuine and tell the truth.
- You might tolerate those who trespass if they are willing to admit to and learn from it.
- You don't allow those who are dishonest; that is something you clearly move away from.

Turning values into boundaries takes practice—and discernment. Some values translate into clear non-negotiables, while others have more flexibility depending on the context. It's not always straightforward, but the more attuned you are to what truly matters to you, the easier it becomes to set boundaries that reflect your sense of integrity.

Setting your boundaries is really about you deciding what works for you and what doesn't. At times, you might let a person cross a boundary because of something else they bring to the relationship. Know that boundary setting is not black and white. There are many shades of gray, all driven by personal preference.

Context is also key.

Your boundaries in a personal relationship might be different from boundaries in a work relationship. Many times, at work, the organizational culture drives environment, so those boundaries come first. You might be able to get by at work with coworkers who don't match up with your values, but the closer you are with someone, the more important it becomes to set and communicate the boundaries that you need for success.

Whatever your values are, converting them into boundaries gives you a basis for living by them in many areas—in relationships, at work, or anywhere else.

That being said, it's not always easy to figure out exactly where the line is. What if you are having trouble finding your boundaries? There are two internal signals that you can pay attention to, indicating that a boundary has been crossed. The first internal signal is anger.

Anger is one of your good friends when setting personal boundaries. It often shows up as a clear signal that a boundary has been crossed or that one of your core values is being compromised. For instance, if you feel angry after being lied to or taken advantage of, it's likely because your value of integrity has been violated.

Anger is a clarifying force[11]—it reveals what matters. It can serve in powerful ways:

- Acting as radar for injustice it helps identify and articulate discrimination or mistreatment.
- As a catalyst for change it can inspire action to address relational harm and shift unhealthy dynamics.
- As a challenge to the status quo, it can motivate necessary upgrades in how you relate—especially when current patterns no longer serve the deeper good of the connection.

The second important warning signal is the *cringe factor*.

I first learned about the cringe factor from Dr. Henry Cloud[12] in his book *9 Things a Leader Must Do*. He describes it as that subtle but unmistakable moment when you feel yourself cringe—maybe you take a deep breath in or feel a tightness in your chest—right before agreeing to something or someone you're not entirely comfortable with. It's easy to brush past, to ignore, to override with logic or politeness. But that cringe? It matters.

It is your body's way of flagging a value conflict. It's a physiological reaction to something that feels off, where your personal values, boundaries, or inner truth are about to be compromised. Maybe it's a request that raises a red flag, a conversation that doesn't feel aligned, or a relationship dynamic that goes against your integrity. That moment of discomfort is your system whispering: *Something here deserves a closer look.*

Instead of pushing through, treat the cringe factor as a sacred pause. Let it be your invitation to stop, check in, and get curious.

Don't take action until you've listened deeply for the gifts the cringe is informing you of. Only then, with your values congruently leading the way is the next step forward meant to happen.

Once you've learned to honor your boundaries and stand for what truly matters most, the next edge of growth to be faced is far more delicate—and more confronting: allowing yourself to receive. Not just love, but support, attention, care, praise, tenderness. This is where many falter. Not because the desire isn't there, but because a deeper belief still lingers—that receiving is unsafe, selfish or underserved. Until that belief is challenged, real intimacy will have trouble taking root.

RECEIVING

The soul should always stand ajar, ready to welcome the ecstatic experience.

— EMILY DICKINSON

Receptivity is another one of those topics that can, for those more independent types, trigger discomfort—what Gay Hendricks calls "upper limiting"[13] in his book *The Big Leap*, and what is sometimes referred to as a "havingness"[14] level. It speaks to the unconscious threshold we each have for how much good we're willing to let in.

This is subtle terrain. Our relationship to receiving isn't formed overnight. If you feel resistance, confusion, or even a blankness as you read, that's not a problem. It's a clue. This section isn't meant to be consumed quickly. Let it work on you. Let it land gently.

To bring this into more conscious awareness, it's important to identify the many ways you might be unwittingly putting up barriers to receiving. This could include love, pleasure, support, or abundance —in the form of intimacy, touch, money, compliments, self-care, or rest. Receiving is a layered and complex topic, so for now, we are going to just take a first pass-through. To fully understand it, we'll begin at the other end of the pool with scarcity.

Ah, scarcity. Few things taste more poignant, pungent, and familiar than its delectable flavor—the bitter taste of not enough and the panicked sensation of impending loss that often follows it.

After my painful divorce, I entered a new relationship, convinced it was love. Prior to it, post divorce, I had become self-sufficient, happy, and fulfilled. However, in that relationship, I compromised my values. I handed over financial control and my needs to the man I expected to be my Prince Charming. Unfortunately, I never let him in on the role he was supposed to play. For eight years, I tried to mold him into someone he wasn't, only to realize he neither had the capacity nor the willingness to meet my desires.

Reflecting on that time, I see that, though I craved connection and intimacy, I lacked the skills to communicate my needs. Unconsciously, I had chosen a partner who couldn't fulfill me, which fed into a deeper pattern of seeking out relationships where I felt devalued. This turned me on, in a strange way, because it allowed me to experience the familiar discomfort of being let down and let go.

I came to understand this as an atrophied "havingness" level—a subconscious limit on how much good I was willing to accept. When I pushed beyond it, I would create reasons to sabotage the situation. Realizing this made me question not just my beliefs, but the core story of who I was.

Through the Men Project—and with my understanding of receiving as a key indicator of transformational growth—I began practicing being open to love and receiving value. Over time, this helped me grow past my scarcity mindset. I learned that we often attract what we unconsciously desire, even if it's negative. Embracing both the light and dark aspects of ourselves can bring us closer to our fullest expression of divinity.

I came to understand that my experience with these incomplete relationships I'd been experiencing were an expression of my own "havingness" level in action—an internal imprint shaped by family, culture, and past experience—that determines how much goodness, sensation, or success you believe you can handle before some part of you unconsciously hits the brakes. When it feels like "too much" or "too good to be true," the system panics, flipping into fight, flight, or freeze, often for reasons that make no sense at first glance. In the moment, it doesn't feel like a limit issue. It just feels like "I suck," or "they suck," or "this will never work." But beneath the story you tell yourself is a nervous system trying to protect you from more than you're accustomed to having.

In other words, the conscious mind "makes up" an unreasonable reason to flip out, one that convincingly hides the actual underlying reason that the flip-out is happening (the unconscious need to avoid too much good stuff), thus keeping the imprint intact and staying in the comfort of the known.

People have all sorts of "havingness" imprints based on the socialized conditioning. Some, for example, are willing to feel high regard through money but are totally unwilling to receive the same level of worth through love, or vice versa. Others become massively activated by the physiological sensations that come with being valued—like being seen, appreciated, and emotionally close.

Your "havingness" level is deeply connected to who you know yourself to be. I say "know" because when it comes to matters of identity, we don't purposefully "believe" ourselves to be something or other; we just feel like we "know" it.

Experiencing a "havingness" level flip out happens when you have hit an internal ceiling for how much goodness—love, success, attention, joy—you can take in while staying present and grounded. When this threshold is breached without awareness, self-sabotage will kick in as a way to restore the familiar sensations and experiences.

For you, this kind of "havingness" level flip-out might look like:

- Complaining or nagging for no real reason
- Picking a fight with someone close to you
- Feeling irritated by someone you usually enjoy being with
- Overeating or oversleeping
- Overanalyzing every little detail

- Feeling entitled ("Well, of course, I have this.")
- Grasping for more when you haven't digested what's present
- Deflecting compliments
- Avoiding intimacy, connection, or touch

These are signs that something good actually might be trying to land, and you aren't yet calibrated to receive it. The work is not to judge yourself, rather, to gently stretch your capacity to stay open and receive when the goodness arrives.

~

The Love Lab Challenge: Try these three practices over the next week to start exploring how to expand your "havingness" level.

1. Accept generosities. Look for opportunities to say yes when others offer to do things for you (e.g., take your groceries out to the car, open the door, buy you a cup of coffee).
2. Ask for what you want. From passing the pepper, to a first-class all-expenses trip to Paris, standing in the value of your desires while flexing your open-hearted capacity is the name of the game.
3. Receive appreciation. Play with just saying "thank you" (full stop), without the need to deflect, explain, or justify.

Receiving can crack you open in unexpected and surprising ways. It sounds beautiful—and it is—but it also requires something you may have been taught to avoid: vulnerability. To truly receive love, you must be willing to be seen. And that can feel terrifying.

Yet, it's only through vulnerability that real love has a place to land.

TRYING ON VULNERABILITY

> *To be fierce and to show mercy toward others; both are acts of immense bravery and greatest necessity. Struggling souls catch light from other souls who are fully lit and willing to show it.*
>
> — CLARISSA PINKOLA ESTÉS

If you at all have done the previous Love Lab Challenges on receiving, you may have landed on some pretty juicy awareness:

Receiving feels vulnerable. To be vulnerable is to feel exposed.

Giving is so much more comfortable—the willingness to support without question is so strong that often one can lose oneself in the giving. It is how you ended up being so successful in your career. Giving allows you to manage, control, and dictate an outcome. You are in charge of what is given. You decide when. You decide how. And it feels good to do so. Experiencing the joy of giving, no matter the motivating factor, is a real, biological thing that psychologists call a "helper's high."[15] Much like a runner's high, the feeling activates the same areas in the brain that other pleasurable activities do.

Vulnerability means stripping away the pretty photos on social media and showing the world your glaring faults. To let someone else inside the world you have created so they can know the real you.

One of the most challenging aspects of doing the real work of Growing Down—the kind that leads to true transformation in your relationships—is allowing yourself to be vulnerable.

Let's begin with what vulnerability is NOT:

- Vulnerability is not weakness.
- Vulnerability is not letting it all hang out.
- Vulnerability is not going it alone.
- Vulnerability is not winning or losing.
- Vulnerability is not good or bad.

Vulnerability is the experience of uncertainty, emotional exposure, and risk (hello: human!) It means consciously choosing to let yourself be seen, rather than hiding your emotions, needs, or desires from others.

In other words, vulnerability is the path to intimacy. It is a radical act of honesty. A willingness to be seen for who you truly are and risk rejection.

If you were raised in a "get 'er done" and "suck it up" environment you have probably built your career success on tenacity and grit. This likely helped you thrive, but didn't teach you how to navigate uncertainty or tolerate emotional risk. The skills required for genuine connection. You've developed habits, embedded deeply, that keep you stifled and bottled up: *Don't be controversial, don't be unique, do anything "crazy" or "stupid" or "selfish."*

It's not safe.

Growing Down is the practice of deliberately putting yourself in positions where you might get rejected, saying a joke that might not land, asserting an opinion that may differ from others, and telling someone that you love them and won't take it back.

Practicing vulnerability really is as simple as just doing these things. And, although being more vulnerable is simple, it rarely is easy. Sticking your neck out emotionally feels risky and there can be consequences to it.

Cultivating your discomfort resilience around vulnerability is a process, not a destination.

∿

The Love Lab Challenge: By now, you've likely begun to notice some of the outdated stories and beliefs that shaped your IOS— ones that may have protected you in the past, but no longer serve the ways in which you approach relationships now.

This exercise is an invitation to meet those beliefs and stories with radical honesty and vulnerability.

Start by naming the ones you've become aware of through this book. Things like:

- I can't trust anyone fully.
- I'm too old/fat for a relationship.
- It's too late for me. That ship has sailed.
- All the good ones are taken.

Ask yourself: Is this true? Does this belief/story support my present need and desire for love or relationship? If not what's a better belief? A better story I can tell?

Be bold. Be kind. Be real. This is the sacred work of Growing Down so you can rise ready to upgrade your IOS to meet the present need.

∿

Growing Down means tending to your roots with consistent, intentional practices that update your functioning to meet present relational needs. It's how you become rooted in your truth—

genuinely, honestly, and with deep trust so you can Grow Up from solid ground.

Growing Down is the essential groundwork for Growing Up—it's what prepares you to enter the dating field with self-trust, clarity and emotional integrity.

The process of Growing Down has you going against the whole drift of culture. It means, among other things, calming your own bad feelings without the help of another, pursuing your own goals, and standing on your own two feet on your own updated terms.

Most associate such skills with singlehood. But a partnership and marriage (if that's the direction your heart feels led to) cannot succeed unless you claim your sense of self *in the presence of another*. The resulting growth from your willingness to engage in the real work of digging down over and again turns right around. It fuels your future or budding relationship. In long-term commitments and marriage, it fuels passionate intimacy and sexual connection. You will find that this newfound comfort level with vulnerability changes things far from your intimate relationships. It pays wide-ranging dividends in domains from friendship to creativity to work.

Ready for your next step?

Let's go!

~

Creative Edge Experience: Metacognitive Drawing—Accessing Insight Through the Pen.

All you need: two pieces of paper and a couple of markers.

Metacognitive Drawing is simply this: thinking *while* your hand is moving. Metacognition means *thinking about your thinking*, and it deepens self-attunement. When you pair this kind of reflection with gentle, repetitive drawing/doodling, you create a pathway for your inner knowing, especially when you sit with a question you don't yet have full clarity on.

It's deceptively simple. However, research shows that within five to seven minutes of drawing or doodling, most people experience a noticeable shift.[16] They become calmer, have more access, and are more aware. This isn't about making art. It's about making contact—with *yourself.* No artistic skill required.

Write the following question along one side of your page: *"What have been my personal barriers to love?"*

- Hold the question gently in your awareness and begin to draw a slow spiral with your dominant hand. Start in one direction, then reverse it.
- Switch hands and color. Let your nondominant hand take over and continue the spirals, changing directions as you go.
- Keep returning to the question softly; no need to force answers.
- Alternate hands and color again, changing directions, keeping the motion fluid, small, and loose.
- When you feel a shift in your state, switch from spirals to another shape: waves, zigzags, loops. Keep alternating hands and direction.
- Let it unfold organically.
- When experience feels complete, draw lines that connect your question to the rest of the image.
- Now pause. On a new sheet of paper, write down any insights, phrases, images, or answers that come through during the process.

This practice helps you hear your own voice more clearly. Let it be easy. Let it surprise you.

PART III
GROWING UP

To be fully seen by somebody, then, and be loved anyhow—this is a human offering that can border on miraculous.

— ELIZABETH GILBERT

Growing up is about becoming wiser in how you step forward with another, not with armor, but with heart. It's about moving from reaction to responsibility while cultivating maturity, emotional resilience, and genuine connection. Here, you don't abandon who you are. Rather, you learn to assess and choose a partnership's capacity for both honoring and co-creating what you both want.

CASE STUDY

> *We accept the love we think we deserve.*
>
> — STEVEN CHBOSKY

Growing up.

This expression might conjure thoughts of leaving childhood behind: becoming responsible, self-sufficient, maybe even hardened. We're taught it means not needing anyone, having it all together, becoming more logical, less emotional, handling things on our own. But in the context of relationships, that idea only gets us partway there.

In the context of this book, Growing Up marks a pivotal turning point. This is where the rubber meets the road. Everything you uncovered, healed, and continue to practice from the Growing Down phase now gets tested—not in theory, but in real time.

Because now, you're adding a new variable: another person.

All of your internal clarity—your self-trust, your values, your boundaries—will be invited into practice as you begin to relate outwardly. This is where your desire meets reality, where independence matures into interdependence. And where your instinct to protect, perform, or prove will try to reassert itself the moment you feel the stakes rise. In other words, this is where it all gets very real.

Many of my clients arrive at this juncture with deep self-awareness yet still find themselves caught in painful relational patterns. Their old story showing up in a new outfit, over and over again.

Let's look at how this plays out.

Meet K.

"I'm currently struggling with the following: The men I find myself most attracted to are, like me, fiercely independent, intelligent, adventurous, interesting, passionate, and funny. Unlike me, the only interest they seem to have in a partner (me) is sexual. The concepts of marriage and children also repel these men. But those are both things I long for. Why would men I have so much in common and chemistry with not want more out of me than sex? Why am I not that 'woman who changes their mind' about commitment?"

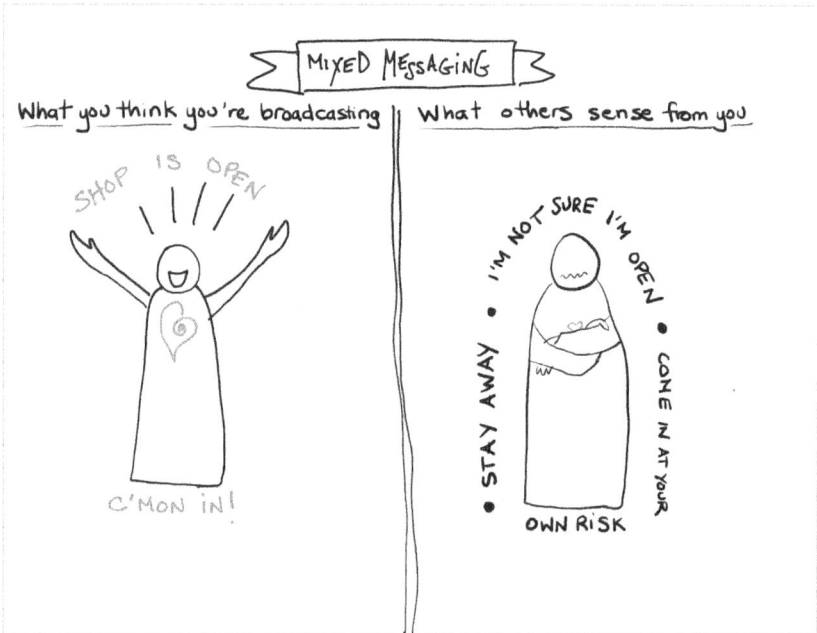

The above scenario is more common than you'd think. It's one I see regularly in my relationship coaching practice. K is a fiercely independent woman attracting fiercely independent men. Embedded within her complaint lies a deeper longing for marriage and children, desires that, at first glance, might seem to contradict that fierce independence.

Two fiercely independent people, one of whom desires dependents and interdependence in the form of marriage. What are the chances of this kind of relationship working out over the long haul? Slim to none.

Let me be clear: I am not advocating that you give up this quality or abandon this strength. Your independence is the very skill that allows you to lead, to innovate, to take risks, to get things done in the world. It is powerful. It is necessary. However, in long-term relationship dynamics, this same strength can unintentionally sabotage intimacy. That being said, if what you are just looking for is a casual connection, carry on.

On the other hand, if what you seek is long-term commitment, partnership, family (or not), your fierce independence sends the opposite message of what you truly desire. And no matter how much you hope, you're unlikely to be the exception who "changes his mind."

> *Until you allow yourself to depend, a partner will not show up as dependable, even if you still expect it from them.*

What K cannot yet see is that her frustration, longing, confusion, and anger are not liabilities. They are gold. They are the source of her power and her clarity. Because she is unaware of this, navigating the tension between her need for independence and her longing for commitment feels insurmountable.

So, how to proceed?

ATTACHMENT PREFERENCE AND FIGURES

We are born in relationship, we are wounded in relationship, and we can be healed in relationship.

— HARVILLE HENDRIX

You may have heard a lot about attachment theory—the idea that our earliest emotional bonds form the blueprint for how we show up in relationships.

Research has found[17] that the personality traits and attachment patterns that will define an individual throughout their life can be clearly identified by the age of seven. As we grow, those personality traits and attachment styles remain recognizable in our adult lives.

When I came across this research early in my personal growth and maturation process, I was taken aback. *What? Do you mean, as an adult, I essentially act like my seven-year-old self when under stress in all relational matters?*

It turns out: yes.

While that knowledge didn't take away the pain of failed relationships, it provided the smoking gun to all my relationship woes. What I discovered, through further research and lived experience, changed everything.

Before we go any further, I feel it is vital to put all of this in context, specifically regarding how the brain works. Understanding the neuroscience gives you a fuller picture of what it takes to break free from old attachment patterns that no longer serve you.

As a human species, we have survived for millennia due to a single imperative: "Thou shall not get killed." Our brain is hardwired, first and foremost, for survival. Its primary function is to ensure we continue living as individuals and as a species. Perceived danger, from a brain perspective, requires fast action—without getting slowed down by the unnecessary details of thinking it through. In other words, if you are standing on a railroad track with an approaching train, you are wired to act first and think later.

However, our brain's survival skills can be at odds with healthy relationships. The part of the brain, the survival part I like to refer to as our "primitives,"[18] our beasts within, doesn't wait for your permission. First in the chain of command with respect to survival. Reflexively they launch into fight, flight, freeze, or fawn before you've even realized what's happening.

Fortunately, we have a more evolved, social part of our brain. In contrast to our warring brain, it functions as our loving brain.

I like to think of this part of the brain as the "ambassadors." It's responsible for reason, emotional regulation, and empathy. This is what your consistent Growing Down practices really empower.

There's a myth that you can't teach an old dog new tricks, that our brains are hardwired and incapable of change. Research on neuroplasticity shows this is not true—that the brain indeed has the capacity to create new neural pathways while repurposing those that are no longer used. What I have shared regarding attachment style does not mean you are locked into those familiar patterns for life. In fact, the contrary is true: Everything can change for you given the correct reframing, mindset mastery, retraining, and consistency.

In childhood, we develop attachments in response to the parent from whom we most needed to earn love. This becomes the blueprint —or imago—we carry into adult relationships.

You may think you've been looking for a partner based on a résumé-style qualities: smart, funny, successful, attractive. But subconsciously, you've been seeking a particular brand of heartbreak— one that mirrors your original attachment wound.

For me, this was my father.

In retrospect, I was drawn to men who were emotionally unavailable, highly intellectual, and pragmatic—a near replica of the connection I had with him. When I would meet emotionally astute and sophisticated men, I didn't feel the "spark." Because chemistry isn't about compatibility—it's about familiarity.

The first step in Growing Up means becoming conscious of this dynamic. It means learning to track the subtle cues of attraction and ask: *Is this love, or this a wound calling out to be healed?*

A Course in Miracles puts it best: "When I am healed, I am not healed alone" (Lesson 137).

The work of attachment theory has value—as it applies to creating an awareness and understanding of default patterns and coping mechanisms established in infancy—to consciously and consistently make choices and take actions in service of a more secure way of being.

Growing Up is what happens when you are conscious of your tendency and add the new variable of a partner.

All the work of Growing Down becomes a dynamic process through which you can be in close proximity with a partner and still maintain a separate sense of self. Space to speak your own mind, think your own thoughts, and attain your own ambitions and dreams while coupled. A space where you can translate your visionary leadership skills into a relationship that is equally groundbreaking. A space to build a Legacy of Love that extends beyond your professional success, offering a sanctuary for emotional connection and a springboard for your mutual dreams.

Rather than reducing partnership to a quest for safety, security, and compensation for childhood disappointments—a trap that actually prevents you from Growing Up—relationships become a cradle of development.

Rather than maintaining an infantilized vantage point, you begin to relate from maturity, presence, and conscious choice. And rather than clinging to exclusive independence, this next stage invites you to explore the strength inherent in *interdependence*.

INDEPENDENCE V. INTERDEPENDENCE

⌘

True independence is not a rejection of connection, but a confident invitation to interdependence.

— ESTHER PEREL

We are taught to be independent, strong and resilient. Not to show any weakness or seek emotional support. It makes sense that this training might make us feel like depending on one another is a terrible thing. Growing Up in love lets you stop confusing strength with self-containment. It reveals real strength as something different.

We humans are tribal. We need each other for survival.

Looking for a partner while simultaneously proving to every potential one that we are entirely self-sufficient, self-reliant, and capable of handling things on our own feels incredibly isolating. And while independence is a beautiful strength, when it becomes armor, it blocks the very connection we are longing for.

As a dating approach, it often backfires—especially when what is truly desired is a partner to lean on. Someone who is trusted for emotional support, responsibility, and a vision of a life built together. If we never allow ourselves to be seen as needing or desiring anything, how can a partner ever feel invited to contribute, care, or show up in a meaningful way?

Let's begin by understanding what interdependence is:

An interdependent relationship is one where a couple acknowledges they're two people who complement each other, as opposed to *completing* each other. They start the relationship from a place of wanting, not needing, an emotional connection.

The key here is differentiation: the ability to stay true to yourself without caving to the pressure to conform to the outdated, unhelpful ways you may have relied on before reading this book. As you begin seeking—and being with—a new partner, the goal is to handle discomfort with a sense of responsibility rather than trying to protect yourself or the relationship from the inevitable changes that intimacy brings. Interdependence is marked by flexibility and a focus on your strengths, not by slipping into familiar patterns of compensating for one another's limitations and unmet needs.

It's easier to be independent when you're alone. Pursuing your own goals and standing up for your desires, beliefs, personal likes, and dislikes in the midst of a relationship is a far tougher feat. Growing Up is an evolutionary mandate: the ability to be known for and loved for being yourself, no matter what.

And it will test you like nothing else.

TRUST THE COMPASS WITHIN

When you stop outsourcing your clarity, and start listening inward, love stops being a maze—and becomes a map.

— JOËLLE LYDON

From the personal experience of healing my own relational wounds and over a decade of research in relationship science, I've learned that our minds and hearts will take us on very distinct paths when it comes to love.

The intention behind testing the rootedness you developed during your Growing Down practices is to support your Growing Up—by entering dating with your heart leading the way. When you do this, you begin to experience a new kind of freedom: freedom from drawing in mismatched partners, and freedom to attract someone who is a perfect match to you.

When K told me she struggled with an attraction to men, who, like her, were fiercely independent, intelligent, adventurous, interesting, and funny, but repelled by marriage and children and only interested in sex, I let her know this was common.

In my relationship coaching practice, I've heard the same story countless times.

The skills you develop to make things happen in the world of your career are not always useful and transferable to relationships. To borrow a saying: When trained to be a hammer, everything looks like a nail. You become a one-trick pony.

When you say, "I'm fiercely independent," the message you send is, "*I don't need you.*" Where's the motivation for a potential partner to put skin in the game?

It is no wonder K's pool is filled with noncommittal men who don't need her either, except for sex, of course. That she identifies as fiercely independent takes them off the commitment hook … leaving her puzzled when she reveals her true desires for marriage and children.

The issue is not her independence. Her identification as such limits her in her ability to fully express the complexities of who she is or what she wants. She wants to receive. She wants to be seen, heard, understood. Gotten. She wants a partner who has her back. But all of these desires live inside her, *unexpressed*.

If you take anything from this book, it's this: You don't get any say in your desires. You do, however, get a say on whether or not to act on them.

One of the ways I support my clients in feeling legitimate about their desires is by having them state their dating purpose upfront, on the very first date. This not only builds your sense of legitimacy and resilience, but it also builds your receiving muscle. It also helps you sort the riffraff from the real deal, more easily identifying those who would be willing to give you what you rightfully want.

K could have shared, "The purpose of my dating is to find a committed, loving partner who desires to marry and have children. What is the purpose of yours?" If their response had been, "I am just looking for a one-night stand," she would have been free to choose to either take them up on their offer or thank them for a lovely evening as they parted ways.

No matter the outcome, by stating your dating purpose, you get to stay true to yourself and your desires instead of getting caught up in doubt, confusion, anger, shame, blame, and frustration. If this approach feels confronting, it is. It flies in the face of what we've been taught about relationships: "Hold your cards close until you get chosen."

In the 1980s singer Pat Benatar had a song entitled "Love Is a Battlefield." Everything we've been taught about our approach to coupling is more akin to a military operation—strategizing, censoring, curating, revealing only certain thoughts and beliefs to position yourself to have the greatest relational advantage.

This is likely the approach you used to climb the career ladder. It worked a treat. However, it will blow up your attempts at finding and co-creating the intimate, honest, genuine, and sincere relationship you desire. The shift begins when you stop bracing for battle and start showing up as an ally, not an adversary.

For men and women to relate as adversaries is in some way a natural outgrowth of men having more power due to size and strength. To counterbalance that, we've been taught to emasculate men. We've:

- Bought into the "Men Are Pigs Culture";
- Criticize, blame, shame, and judge them covertly or overtly;
- Tease them like their male friends would (except with a knife buried inside it);
- Withhold participation (i.e., sex, conversation);
- Cut them off;
- And worst of all: Believe the story that nothing they can do will make you happy. This is like a cancer.

These mindsets and beliefs are what kept me in a perpetual cycle of attracting mismatched partners. If you continue to struggle, return to the practices outlined in Growing Down as you progress through this section of the book. Know that Growing Down and Up are both/and propositions—you needn't wait until you are perfectly "fixed" to get started.

In that Growing Down work, you begin to shift your relational approach from adversary to ally. When engaged in the Men Project I learned to not hold all my cards close but rather have the courage to lay them all on the table. In doing so, I learned to drop my defenses. It was this that allowed me to change my mind about men and what it meant to be in relationship with them. It gave me the courage to honor my deep desire for love—just as *Mamie* and *Pepère* had.

Get clear. Who are you looking to partner with? Hopefully, a person on the same side, an ally, someone to have your back in challenging and joyful times. Someone to share the profits and the risks.

In the process of Growing Up when assessing whether a partner is a true fit, you want to look for one singular quality. When you are considering sharing in the risks as allies, TRUST is essential.

Honestly, true partnership is impossible with someone you cannot trust. And that trust doesn't begin with the other person. It starts within. When you do the "real" work of approval, of legitimizing your own desires, you begin to cultivate a great sense of peace and trust in your own ability to act on what matters most to you.

~

The Love Lab Challenge: Answer the following questions. They will support you in having more clarity about your TRUE desires (the ones you just can't help but have been withholding until now) and assess if the person you are currently dating possesses the ONE quality of TRUST that you need for the long-term. If you are not currently dating, assess your last partner as a litmus test. Believe me, it will reveal gobs. Don't skip this step. You can thank me later.

1. Get CLEAR: What is your dating purpose? For example:

- Are you looking to be married?
- Have children?

- Co-habitate before making the full commitment move?
- No marriage at all?
- Separate places?

2. ASSESS your dating partner.

- Do you trust them? Why? Why not
- Is this someone you think **you could trust**? (You are not going to be compelled to do this.)

If you don't trust, you won't stand a chance at the following steps; there's still work for you to do in the Growing Down end of things.

TRIGGER WARNING:
REWRITE THE STORY

>
> *If we feel deeply, as we encourage ourselves and others to feel deeply, we will, within that feeling, once we recognize we can feel deeply, we can love deeply, we can feel joy, then we will demand that all parts of our lives produce that kind of joy.*
>
> — AUDRE LORDE

As the saying goes "What you resist, persists." That's why the pattern of mismatched relationships has been a cycle for you. The way to break this cycle is NOT to resist change. This is where your devotion to setting parameters becomes your greatest advocate and teacher—a wellspring for deep wisdom, a gift from the Universe for your deepest liberation, and a most profound and loving connection.

You say you desire to be with that one ideal person who, in your mind, is "out there." The perfect match you seek. But running alongside that desire are quieter, often unspoken beliefs and stories that question whether finding a just-right partner is actually possible for you.

Foot on the gas and the brakes simultaneously, you feel the constriction between wanting what you want and not believing you can have it. So long as this conflict remains unresolved, you will continue to have the experience of getting involved with people who are happy to confirm those beliefs for you.

Have you noticed?

I spent decades in that particular version of hell: frustrated, angry, mistrusting, judging, blaming others (but mostly myself), and feeling like a victim to my desire for Love. When I finally took a stand for what I said I wanted, invested in it, and received support, when I finally engaged in the real work of approval and legitimacy, everything changed.

There is an ancient saying that states, "Nothing ever happens without an onlooker." And, indeed, there's profound power in being witnessed. To be seen—not for who you are pretending to be, but for who you truly are beneath the defenses—is a sacred kind of medicine. When you're doing the deep work of updating the outdated internal and relational operating systems, it's easy to doubt yourself, to lose momentum, or to fall back into old patterns disguised as progress. That's where having a trusted witness, a coach, is invaluable.

A skilled coach doesn't just listen. They reflect your truth back to you when you've forgotten, name what's hiding from view, and hold you lovingly accountable to the version you say you desire.

The supply of what you desire is inexhaustible and unfailing when you become a clear match for it. That being said, choosing to be in a relationship will bring up all your shit. You know this feeling—the way a single look, a familiar mannerism, or a comment that hints at intimacy or a shared future can suddenly activate you, especially when things are just beginning. We drag trauma and old wounds from past relationships into current situations all the time. This is why, if you're looking to find a partner who is the right match, it's imperative that you do the real relational work of Growing Down first, honoring your piece of the Red Thread.

So, when those emotions seemingly appear out of nowhere while in the midst of a new relationship (or even a long-term one), it's time to acknowledge that an old operating system just got activated in you.

Take this beautiful opportunity to upgrade it to meet your current need.

Rather than blowing up a relationship or running away, stay with it and assess if it is even a viable one—not from fear or fantasy, but from a place of clarity and self-trust. When you stay, you create space to course correct. You begin to respond instead of react. And in doing so, you reclaim the power to move forward consciously, instead of numbing out or, worse, slipping back into the habit of armoring up.

Because here's what most of us forget in those moments: You cannot selectively numb out emotions. When you numb out pain, you also numb out joy. The process of readying for love and intimacy demands that you be willing to feel every single emotion as if they were the eighty-eight keys on a piano. Without judgment, allow them all to be played through you.

Our culture does not make room for the full range of our emotional capacity to be expressed. Not all emotions are deemed "acceptable." In a world where logic and reason are valued, the messiness of emotions is not only an inconvenience but also perceived as a lack of control, a personal defect.

Perhaps if we gave each feeling appropriate airtime instead of stuffing it down, we'd feel less fragmented, disconnected, disenfranchised, and depressed. Perhaps if you showed every delicious face you own, people who aren't a match to you might just fall away. ... *Sound dangerous?*

When you cut off what you feel on one end of the spectrum, you limit what you have the bandwidth to feel at the other end. You deny the ones who do have the ability to handle it the honor and pleasure of loving, appreciating, and holding you in that spot. The lie of controlling feelings is that it makes you seem stronger, when in truth, it is actually vulnerability that creates real closeness.

This lie fuels anger. (Did you ever notice the word "danger" includes the word *anger*?) Anger is the gateway to clarity. Let it reveal what you care deeply about.

∾

The Love Lab Challenge: One way to begin playing with your full range of emotions is to clear the clutter of all the stories, superstitions, thoughts, and emotions that clog your mental space. This includes your rage. Take the following practice to your journal. Pen to paper. If you find yourself resisting, remember this: On the other side of your resistance lies what matters most to you. Drop the armor. *What are you angry about?* Allow yourself to answer this question, stream of consciousness. Take it to a confessional of sorts. Because it's a confessional without consequences. Let it all out. Be as childish as possible. Expletives are absolutely welcome! Don't hold back.

STOP CATCHING, START CONNECTING

Vulnerability is the birthplace of love, belonging, joy, courage, empathy, and creativity.

— BRENÉ BROWN

In addition to shifting your relational mindset from adversary to allies, and dropping your armor to feel the full range of emotions available to you, what's required as part of the Growing Up process is another, perhaps new and unfamiliar, approach: *shifting from a catch strategy to an engaging and expressing one.*

The catch strategy might feel second nature to you—it's the approach you may have relied on to get what you want, set yourself up for success, and plan for the next step. This strategy is outwardly focused, like a carefully orchestrated military operation, maneuvering all the pieces into the most advantageous position before taking action. While effective in other areas (such as your career), it's also what keeps the cycle of attracting mismatched partners active.

Why? Because the strategy hides your vulnerability.

Engaging and expressing, on the other hand, requires something radically different: a willingness to reveal. It's about showing your hand, sharing the contents of your heart, and allowing the soft animal of your body—your deepest and truest desires—to speak. Vulnerability here isn't weakness; its strength born of trust, honesty, sincerity, and genuine connection.

Strategy hides. Vulnerability reveals.

And while strategy might win battles and earn you gold stars, it also silences the voice within that longs to love and be loved genuinely. To break this cycle, you must let go of the plan and dare to let your heart be seen and felt.

Here's the other thing: Your catch strategy has you posturing disingenuously in dating. *It makes you start all relationships with a lie.*

Lying is as old as the hills. Still, most everyone hates being told a lie or finding out they have fallen for one. There are bald-faced lies, exaggerations, white lies, lies of omission, false advertising, and promises that become lies. Most lies are an expression of fear, a sense of scarcity, a need for approval, self-protection, or a striving for status.

Lying is also an instinctual response to the real and perceived life and death survival experience. It's no wonder we keep attracting mismatched partners. Too often who your dates are dating and being attracted to is **not actually us**. A facsimile rather than the truth of who we are.

Ask yourself. Have you started every single relationship with a lie? Do you want to stop?

How is the essential ingredient of TRUST meant to be built in your relationship?

The thing about trust is that it's not given—it's revealed. It emerges as the natural outcome of repeated truth-telling, consistent emotional presence, and the courage to be genuine. And it begins with self-trust. That is what the Growing Down process is about: cultivating a relationship with yourself that includes listening to your own intuition and knowing, honoring your boundaries with clarity and grace, and acting in alignment with what you most value.

Only from this rooted place within is it possible to trust another—not blindly, not as a fantasy. You build trust by observing how you are responded to in your emotional truth, your vulnerability, honesty, sincerity, and your desire to be fully seen.

Trust is the invisible current that allows love to circulate safely between two people. Without it, love struggles to take root. Connection can't deepen, and intimacy is unable to grow. Safety isn't a luxury in love—it's the soil love grows in.

This is why it's imperative to stop reacting to what you think someone else wants. Stop positioning yourself in the most flattering light, being careful, while strategically concealing the truth of who you are. Stop adapting to other people when it just sells you out. Stop lying.

It means going against your instinct for survival. One of the highest achievements is our ability to think critically, to actively and consciously regulate our nervous system, make choices that are in service of a greater good. This is the Red Thread in action.

In truth, you are not beholden to your instincts. Take the time to put into practice what's needed to Grow yourself Down, no matter what.

Start expressing and engaging. Become the person who is being responded to:

- Be yourself.
- Say what you want.
- Share what you're up to.
- And let others react to that.

Dating is not a "finding problem." *It's a sorting process.*

Expressing and engaging become very efficient ways to sort. Those who like your honesty will stay. Those who don't will go away and set you free. You must be vigilant in chasing off your scarcity thinking: *What if none of them like me? What if there IS no one else?*

Let me remind you that TRUST is the key element to long-term relationships. This is where your Growing Down practices come in play. Return to them over and over again while in the throes of the Growing Up process. It will be a lifesaver. And, even if you are currently single, the practice of developing self-trust as a skill will pay you back in spades when you've found a partner that is a match.

◦◦◦

The Love Lab Challenge: Dropping the Lies. Take the following questions to your journal. Put pen to paper. Allow yourself to, as Rilke would say, "Go to the limits of your longing." And "Let everything happen to you: beauty and terror."

- If you were TRULY yourself on your dates, what would you express that you normally withhold?
- If you were "naughty," "bad," or "irreverent," what would you dare risk expressing?

GIVE UP FALSE ADVERTISING

Be yourself—everyone else is already taken.

— OSCAR WILDE

If your dating desire and purpose are to be wildly authentic AND to be loved with no risk, then this book is probably not for you. However, if you sense there is a different way, know that your current approach has not yielded what you want, and you are willing to give it a try … *stay with me, here.*

We may never have met, you and I. And I have been doing this work long enough to imagine that you want your dating and relationships to be an expression of your heart. You want to be with someone with whom it feels safe being honest, genuine, and sincere. Someone you can trust brings out your genuineness—and that's the person you say "yes" to.

Here's the jiggy: When you pursue a partner because of sexual attraction and chemistry, it is difficult to be sincere. Your "catch strategy" and your scarcity mindset will become activated. You will believe that you have to have *that* partner. After all, you think, they may be "The One!"

What, then, does it mean to be truly genuine? What are the things worth revealing with honesty and sincerity? Two ways to get started:

1. **Your dating purpose.** Where you see your dating going as far out as you can see, you're looking for the long-term track.
2. **Your deal-breakers.** This is what stops relationships and where many give themselves up. Relationships sink from the holes that were there from the beginning. Fly the flag of deal-breakers from the outset:

- Children
- Religion
- Drug and alcohol use
- Lifestyle choices
- Smoking
- Money
- When/whether to get married

When you choose to be courageously genuine, those who are not a match become glaringly obvious. They are not a fit for what you desire, truly. So, move on. Keep sorting until you meet the one who is.

If your mind screams at the prospect of opening your kimono from the very first date, your instinct is playing you. By regulating your nervous system, you get to claim sovereignty over your relational future. You get to stand in your value, honor your desire, not short-change yourself, or settle for less than you deserve.

It's simple, not easy. Overcoming fear and scarcity is a choice. Especially when there's fear that the person you're dating will go away, that no one will step into that spot, and there's a chance you will die forever alone. We're taught, conditioned, socialized, and instinctively believe that if we are not truly genuine, we won't be hurt. If we don't make ourselves vulnerable, we won't experience pain. And thus, we create fewer opportunities for things to turn out well. Long-suffering only prolongs the hurt without bringing you any closer to the love you truly want.

Everything wonderful that happens in a relationship happens because those involved choose to be vulnerable.

I'm going to share something with you that might feel controversial: You're always going to be attracted to someone who drives you crazy. It's not a flaw in your picker—it's by design. The partner you're drawn to often mirrors an original attachment wound, offering you the opportunity to face and transform it. But here's the deeper truth: As long as your relationship serves as a sanctuary for emotional connection and a springboard for mutual dreams, why would you ever want to leave?

The purpose of a conscious relationship isn't to complete or fix you. It's to help you fall more in love with yourself and your life. Don't misunderstand me. Not every moment will be unicorns and rainbows. You will not fall more in love with yourself every moment of every day. If fifty-one percent of the time you're expanding, healing, laughing, loving—and choosing each other—it's a win. All you need is fifty-one percent to round up to a hundred.

Still looking for the fairy-tale ending? This is probably not your book. I'm probably not the coach for you. If you're looking to put skin in the game, no longer deny your true desires (after all, you have no say in what you want), but lay claim to them fully and stay with your relationship for the next leg of the commitment adventure, keep reading.

You'll be shown the next phase of relational mastery: Growing Together, where, once you've committed to partnership, you'll gain navigational certainty for your relationship long-term.

∼

Creative Edge Experience: Face What You're Avoiding—A Drawing Exercise for Brave Awareness. Sometimes, when we grow, we might feel resistance. It's possible that something in the Growing Up section of this book stirred discomfort, fear, or a quiet "nope, not going there." This practice is an invitation to meet your resistance with compassion, creativity, and curiosity.

You'll need:

- Your phone camera
- Two blank sheets of paper
- A black permanent marker
- A colored pencil

Follow these steps:

1. Take a photo of yourself with your **eyes closed**.
2. On the first page of paper, use your dominant hand to draw a single line drawing of your face from the photo. Do not lift the pen. The output will not really look like you … and that's the point.
3. When done, pause and ask: *What am I avoiding?* Let your inner voice respond. Use the colored pencil to write what comes up inside the drawing.
4. On the second page, using your nondominant hand, create another single line drawing of your face from the photo. Again, no lifting the pen. This will feel awkward. Let it.
5. Now, using the colored pencil, fill that face—every space and shape—with the worries and fears you have around the topic you're avoiding. Let the pencil speak your truth.
6. Open the eyes on the second drawing by redrawing them (with your marker) as open. Then, from this "brave, opened-eye self," write down the brave message it wants you to hear.

PART IV
GROWING TOGETHER
(AND FLOURISHING)

The effect of transparent communication is the power to illuminate that field, infusing its byways and interstices with the light and lucidity of awareness, to bring healing and repair to the collective.

— THOMAS HÜBL

Growing Together is where love stops being just a feeling and becomes a daily practice. It's an invitation to reimagine conflict, communication, and commitment—not as obstacles but as sacred opportunities. The work of co-creating something larger than yourself: your Sacred Third. A space that is strong enough to hold both your individuality and your deep connection, and thrive within your relationship long-term.

RELATIONSHIP AS THE SACRED THIRD ENTITY

I want you to consider that the minute you enter into a relationship, there are now three entities: you, the other person, and the relationship.

— TEAL SWAN

The relationship I have with my husband is unusual.

Not because it's perfect. Not because we avoid conflict. Because it's conscious. From the beginning, it felt unfamiliar—not in a way that created fear; rather in the way that it stirred an ancient knowing. On some unconscious level, we knew that the first guiding principle of the Red Thread, "I belong" was at play—we were already connected. And there was nothing to lose.

The first, "I love you" I shared with him, was quickly followed by, "and I won't take it back."

Together, we co-created a relationship expectation of impeccability with word and deed, of vulnerability and transparency. Honesty, sincerity, and truth were the values we both wanted to uphold. We consciously wanted these tenets to be the foundation upon which to build a relationship. Even if this relationship were not to work out.

For this, we honored the guiding principle of "I'm responsible" for our own part of the Red Thread. I saw this as a practice of learning how to, brick by brick, create the kind of relationship that I had always desired. I wanted to optimize my ability to learn from it for the next one, if there were to be a next one. Remaining open, curious, and detached I fully leaned into transparency and receiving.

Along the way, we each stood at various crossroads to check, "Are you still in?" As we did, making no assumptions and witnessing one another in the process, each "yes" transitioned us from dating to exclusivity to full-on commitment. We recognized the magic inherent in the unknown and in this adventure. Each time, we chose to be in a more committed relationship—letting love guide our decision. We built trust with one another—after experiencing our unique previous heartbreak.

"US" became the center point of our choices.

Over a decade ago, he started off as research ... today, he still is.

In constructing a covenant of safety and trust, we agreed to hold one another's hearts honestly for safekeeping while we each worked on healing our own personal wounds. Our relationship has, and continues to, remake us. The work of Growing Together is never a one-and-done. Our commitment to one another means we've agreed to the discipline of putting the needs of our relationship above our own.

In my work and personal life, I see relationships as a meeting of two entities which go on to create a third entity—the Relationship. This is what I've called the Sacred Third.

The process of upgrading your personal IOS and upgrading your relational system means consistently honoring the needs of Sacred Third. Through my work, I have grown to understand that this third entity, the relationship itself—the "we" and "us"—is an intelligent, conscious being with desires, needs, wants, life force, and its own evolutionary trajectory. It requires the right environment to grow and thrive. It's your *responsibility* to nurture it if you wish it to be a viable being.

When clients first consider working with me, they believe our coaching will be exclusively about two people—them and the person they wish to be coupled with or them and their current partner. Stuck in duality, a form of binary thinking, they bring their own personal agendas, life experiences, anxieties, values, beliefs, and traumas to the coupling.

This binary approach places in the center, not what's best for the "US," but the wants and wounds of each individual. It sets up the relationship into an adversarial dynamic, erecting oppositional camps where one agenda is pitted against the other. Where there is a right way, a wrong way, or the highway. A sense of separation—of not feeling seen, heard, understood—then becomes the primary experience.

This results in patterns of control, anger, indifference, passive-aggression, resignation, withdrawal, depression, desperation, or manipulation. Reasons to blame, shame, judge, and criticize the other.

However, when you shift your perspective, viewing the relationship as a third entity, this lose-lose dynamic can shift into a collaborative co-creation in service of the next level of relational upgrade. You can create a more generative and fruitful outcome that benefits *all involved*.

Moving from a dual "me-you" vantage point to one that acknowledges the existence of a third entity at play—Relationship—one with its own energy and form, allows for a common lens and focus, especially when challenges arise.

**Relationship = person A + person B + Sacred Third entity
(the relationship between person A & B)**

Adopting a "we-us" mindset means you aim to not only nurture and support one another, but the Relationship itself. Bringing Relationship as the Sacred Third element is to rise above your own individuality to look beyond your own egoic needs for the good of all.

Just as though it were a person, this Sacred Third entity has its own lifespan and vitality, whether weak or strong, loving or cynical. It provides an objective way to examine and evaluate your relationships with others, independent of how you FEEL about them. It lets you see the relationship *as it really is.*

Paying attention to, watering, pruning, and nurturing it with honesty, openness, curiosity, and connection allow Trust and Faith to grow as Love is the consistent decision made in its service.

> *Co-creating a long-term relationship and Love is not for the faint of heart.*

The caring and feeding of your Sacred Third demands presence, attention, respect, appreciation, vulnerability, humility, and a willingness to take full responsibility for your piece of the Red Thread.

In her book, *A Return to Love*, Marianne Williamson shares, "Part of working on ourselves, in order to be ready for a profound relationship, is learning how to support another person in being the best that they can be. Partners are meant to have a priestly role in each other's lives.

They are meant to help each other access the highest parts within themselves."

Co-agreeing to adopt this relational stance will open your heart wide. Not only will it continue to individually Grow you Down, deepening your personal root system, it will anchor you in moments of adversity.

Becoming a couple who honors the Sacred Third as the agreed relational culture and foundation means that no situation, person, or circumstance has the capacity to tear you apart. Instead, these tests make you stronger together.

Every conflict is worth the risk for the gifts it provides.

THE EDGES OF POTENTIALITY

❦

A threshold is not a simple boundary; it is a frontier that divides two different territories, rhythms, and atmospheres. Indeed, it is a lovely testimony to the fullness and integrity of an experience or a stage of life that it intensifies toward the end into a real frontier that cannot be crossed without the heart being passionately engaged and woken up.

— JOHN O'DONOHUE

Years ago, as my husband and I gazed over our backyard, he casually shared that the space in nature with the most potentiality and fecundity is found at the edges. For example, where our open lawn meets the surrounding forest. In ecology, this has been referred to as the *edge effect,*[19] which represents the explosion of life that happens when two ecosystems collide.

These edges allow the mixing of water, soil, seed, light, and nutrients, which not only promote plant growth but also attract insects, which in turn attract birds that eat the insects and plants, providing fertilizer and dispersing more seeds. Resources accumulate. New species emerge. Energy multiplies, promoting the interaction of different niche species. Edges are where transformation thrives.

As in nature, so in the relational world.

Relationships have edges, too. They are the threshold places where your individuality meets your partner's. Where bonds are deepened, new possibilities explored, and hidden potentials unlocked. They are also where your upbringing rubs up against theirs. Where your ways of thinking, loving, reacting, and dreaming bump into each other. They are the places where sameness ends and differences begin. These are not signs of failure or incompatibility. They are signs of potentiality.

And just like in nature, these places are alive.

It's easy to feel safe in sameness, in the known. But real intimacy grows in the in-between—the generative space of discomfort. Just like in nature, edges in relationships are where new possibilities are born. New insights made. New growth gained. New connection created.

Too often, we're taught to fear the edges. We're told love should feel seamless, easy, and aligned at all times. But in truth, edges are where intimacy deepens—if we're willing to stay present. Edges are not something to manage or smooth other. They are something to tend.

The edges are where you're invited to listen more deeply. To witness yourself and your partner more fully. To allow new understanding and growth to take root in the space between your togetherness.

The Sacred Third lives here.

It's in the threshold—the in-between—where something larger than either of you can emerge. New relational dynamics. New patterns. New ways of seeing. New possibilities for connection that neither of you could have created alone.

Though at times uncomfortable, it is always fertile.

And while some edges appear as expansion and inspiration, others will emerge as friction, misunderstanding, misalignment, or challenge. That, too, is part of the edge's terrain. When you learn to recognize those moments not as threats, but as an invitation, you begin to walk together with more grace and less fear. The more fluency you build around navigating those edge spaces, the more resilient your relationship becomes.

Especially when those edges sharpen into conflict, you can meet them with love, clarity, and presence rather than panic or collapse. Learning to take full responsibility for your part in unhelpful relationship dynamics and learning to meet there not with fear, but with clarity, love, and presence, is what will enable your edges to be fruitful on a consistent and ongoing basis.

TAKING 100% RESPONSIBILITY FOR 50% OF THE RELATIONSHIP

Expectations are resentments under construction.

— ANNE LAMOTT

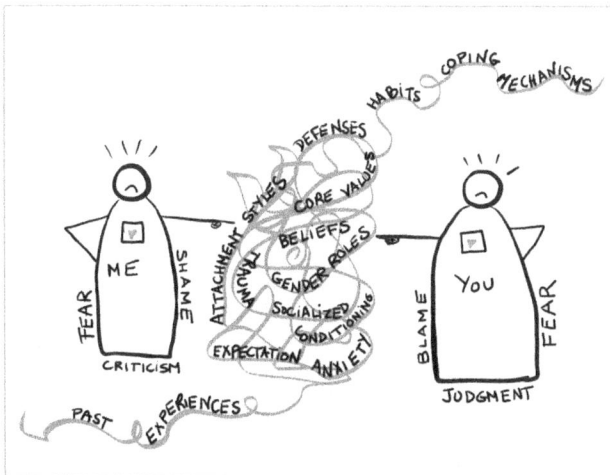

In the complex world of relationships, a profound truth often overlooked serves as the foundation for true mastery: Self-awareness and full personal and energetic responsibility are key to successful connections. As a seasoned coach, I've had the privilege of guiding countless clients on their journey from surface-level romance to profound, lasting love.

Harville Hendrix and Helen LaKelly Hunt, esteemed authors of *Getting the Love You Want*, emphasize the significance of taking one hundred percent ownership of fifty percent of any relational equation.[20] Whether it's navigating a divorce, resolving professional conflicts, enduring heartbreak from a breakup, or reconciling with your child, George Bernard Shaw's quote rings true: "The single biggest problem in communication is the illusion that it has taken place."

Undoubtedly, accepting one hundred percent responsibility for half of any situation can be daunting, especially when emotions are raw. However, it's an essential first step toward personal growth and nurturing healthier, enduring relationships.

The great news is that this is a teachable skill.

Shifting from blame, shame, or making others wrong to embracing personal responsibility is the real work of relationship building. It requires upgrading our beliefs, shedding those of our formative years, and embracing updated, relevant ones that meet the present needs. This transformation empowers us to engage with others based on relational intelligence and competency. Failing to do so is like trying to cut your lawn with a pair of scissors. While certainly you could cut grass that way, it is ineffective, laborious, time-consuming, and plain exhausting.

Feeling stuck can occur when we avoid our emotions, feel inadequate, and allow shame, fear, guilt, anger, and/or stress to keep us from taking the actions needed to move toward more relational competence.

Strong, lasting partnerships are built on mutual actions and discerned responses. When you take ownership of your part in the equation, you empower not only yourself but also enable others to learn from the past. It's a shift from "me" and "you" to the higher ground of "US," where the relationship itself takes precedence.

Our world is calling for a transformation in the way we relate to one another. Geopolitics, wars, climate change, the loss of life, and biodiversity all signal the need for change. One of the reasons I am driven to do the relational work that I do is that I envision a world transformed through *recognizing the Sacred in all beings*. This includes our precious planet.

By taking one hundred percent responsibility for fifty percent of our problems, you can pave the way for more fulfilling and enduring connections. This clarity empowers you to heed the sacred call of relational maturity for the greater good of us all.

CRAZY ON PURPOSE

❧

We are born in relationship, we are wounded in relationship, and we can be healed in relationship.

— HARVILLE HENDRIX

Oftentimes, what we do with partners is to use them as our attachment figure—the person you go to feel safe and soothed.

When you were little, you had a guardian, and they were the safe place you went to whenever you were spooked or scared or confused. You got support, or not. That person became your bonded attachment figure. It's coded in your mind that this figure is the place to go for soothing, safety, and rescuing when the world feels overwhelming.

As a young child, you're not born with the ability to regulate your nervous system to calm yourself down. No child knows how to self-soothe. They are dependent on the caretaker's nervous system, usually their mother, and are entrained to it. When the mother's nervous system calms down, so can that of the child.

Parents, being what they are, are imperfect in lots of ways. The extent that the parent figure is able to calm themselves becomes the extent to which the child can do so. Children feel safe—or not—based on how their parents regulate their own nervous systems. Over time, this becomes the child's baseline for what a regulated state feels like. For better or worse, our caregivers create shape our internal definition of safety.

As an adult, when you are in a committed relationship, your partner, unbeknownst to you, becomes your new attachment figure. And all the imprints, patterns, the good, the bad, and the ugly from your original attachment figure transport right over to them.

So, you're in your relationship.

You're upset. You're fighting, and you get angry. You expect your partner to say and do the things that you've always wanted your original attachment figure to do to make you feel better.

Except they don't.

You don't feel seen, heard, understood—and when they don't do the thing you're hoping for, a sense of entitlement comes into play:

- *Well, they should just hug me.*

- *They should just say it's going to be okay.*
- *They should just be able to talk it through with me.*
- *They should just give me space.*
- *They should just calm down.*
- *They should get angry.*

There may be a variety of things you might think your partner should do in a time such as this. The reason you might feel angry and expect them to do the thing you want is that a little part of you just got activated by their lack of "correct" response to the situation. That little part of you is saying: *Please, attachment figure, rescue me. Soothe me. Help me feel safe right now.*

The reality is that your partner is looking at you as a grown-up adult, probably thinking the same thing: *Why don't YOU rescue me? Soothe me? Help me feel safe right now?*

The trick here is to remember you're no longer a child; you're an adult. Your partner's job is NOT to rescue you, or create a sense of somatic safety, or do whatever it takes to help you calm down. An adult is defined by the realization, the understanding, the knowing that there is no one coming to save you. It's YOUR job to create radical safety in your own body. It's your responsibility.

That's what a grown-up is.

One of the most confronting truths in a relationship is this: No one is coming to save you. Not even the person you love most. Especially not them.

Falling in love and choosing commitment often brings with it a sudden, disorienting realization: The very partner we thought would finally offer only the love we longed for ends up mirroring, almost exactly, the wound we hoped they'd heal. And this isn't by mistake.

Whether deliberately or unconsciously, we tend to choose partners who will replicate the heartbreak with the parent we had to work the hardest to earn love from. It's familiar. It's almost magnetic. And, it holds within it the potential for massive growth. We reach for someone we hope will soothe the ache, and we're handed a mirror instead.

But here's the gift of that recognition—this is our opportunity to grow up in love. Not just grow older, more skilled at navigating conflict, but to mature emotionally in the deepest way—an invitation to become our own internal attachment figure. To parent ourselves. And in so doing, we access the parts of us that know how to tend to the sacred, confused, overwhelmed parts of ourselves without outsourcing that job to our partners (which is unfair anyway, right?). We get to reach, over and again, to our inner ideal caregiver—the one that says "I've got you. I hear you. I won't let you down." That is the intent of self-nurturing and emotional regulation.

And it's truly the most romantic thing you can learn to do in a romantic relationship.

A friend recently came to me upset about her sister-in-law's unreliability. She'd been promised a return call that never came. Instead of speaking to the hurt that lay beneath, she engaged in an offensive weapons approach to get the relationship back on track: criticism and contempt.

Criticism: *"She said she would call me back but didn't."* (Complaint about her character.)

Contempt: *"What's wrong with her? She's such a ____."* (Name-calling and sarcasm.)

Beneath all that grumbling, I heard something else. A quiet, truer message: *I don't matter.* Rather than feel and admit to that vulnerable truth, she did what most people do when we sense a stop in the flow of love: She blamed. She made the other person wrong. Not because it was the most effective response, but because it was the most familiar to her. This way, she got to feel righteous instead of raw.

Blame is often a shield. It lets us avoid the tender ache of perceiving we matter less than we hoped. It distracts us from grief—keeping the deeper healing out of reach. But if we stay with it—are brave enough to feel it—something shifts. We stop outsourcing our worth. We begin to regulate ourselves and we step into the quiet, beautiful responsibility of loving ourselves well—all signatures of ongoing Growing Down work.

When I asked her what it would take to "approve" of her sister-in-law, she was confused.

Approve?

When we disapprove of individuals who don't show up in the way we expect, even when they've never done so before, we set ourselves up to experience the pain of "not mattering" over and over again. In this way, we continue to confirm our innate sense of worthlessness, a pattern we have only too accustomed to.

This pattern is often rooted in the family of origin. You may have learned to contort yourself emotionally, trying to earn love or approval from caregivers who were inconsistent, distracted, or unavailable. Like one of the Matryoshka dolls nestled inside your lineage, you inherited this way of being—layered, shaped, and passed down through generations.

And, there's another way forward.

By choosing to see others as they are, not as you wish them to be rather how they've consistently shown themselves to be, you offer one of the most generous gifts of love: approval without conditions. You get to see them in their innocence. Even when they fall asleep at the wheel of your relationship. Even when they forget how to care for the connection. Even when they fail you.

Don't get me wrong. This doesn't mean you allow yourself to be mistreated. Only that you stop expecting a different outcome from someone who's never had the tools to give it. And, from that clarity, you're free to choose your next move from a place of self-worth instead of self-abandonment.

Toward the end of his life, learning to meet my father with approval rather than expectation was the most genuine way I knew how to be. It became an honest way to relate to him. We didn't get a fairy-tale ending—not even close—but found a more peaceful place with one another. And when he died, there were no regrets.

It's a big leap.

Those willing to engage fully in the work of Growing Down and Growing Up will experience a natural, subtle but powerful shift: the beginning of a natural, steady flow of love—not one borne of perfection, performance, but of loving presence. You begin to accept others as they are—not because they've finally changed, but because you've stopped needing them to. You begin to accept yourself, too—not as a fixed or flawless human, but as one worthy of love even in the midst of your own process of becoming.

By no means does this mean you abandon your boundaries or standards. It means you stop waging war with *what is*. You stop trying to fix others as a strategy to feel safe, managing every interaction like it's a survival test, clinging onto the idea that if they would just change, you could finally relax and be happy.

When you drop the need to blow up their village or run for the hills—you allow yourself to stand still in love. You begin to relate instead of react. And from this grounded place ... you get to grow *together*.

This kind of love—enduring, courageous, real—invites a new internal posture. One that says: *I can see limitations (yours and mine) and still choose compassion. I can witness the sleepwalking (yours and mine) and still hold onto myself with dignity. I can love you without losing me.*

When you apply this lens as a core practice, you start to understand that approving of others doesn't mean agreeing with their behavior. It means refusing to outsource your sense of safety, worth, or emotional harmony to their ability to show up a certain way. This is the foundation of courageous love—how intimacy and resilience is built. And perhaps most importantly: This is how the inherited pattern of innate worthlessness stops with you.

When you choose to see yourself and others through these eyes you break the cycle. You become the one who no longer demands perfection as a prerequisite for love, and become the one who can give what you never received:

Unwavering love, steady presence, and the permission to grow—together.

And what a Legacy of Love you get to leave as a result.

RUN TOWARD THE DANGER

The purpose of a relationship is to help each individual fall more in love with themselves and their life. Not every moment gives you the opportunity to experience this with your partner—but you want to be doing so more often than not.

(After all, you just need fifty-one percent to round up to a hundred.)

Where one partner will emphasize individuality, autonomy, and selfhood more, the other will lean more toward togetherness, connection, and "we." Successful long-term relationships strike a balance between those two essential polarities.

Both aspects are as vital to each individual and to the relationship as breathing. The "in breath" is the togetherness, the "we" energy, while the "out breath" is individuality, the "me" space.

Together. Apart.

Both qualities are equally valuable and necessary, for each individual and for the partnership as a whole.

In a thriving partnership, one person tends to safeguard the sacred bond of togetherness, a quality thought leader Annie Lalla refers to as "othering." The other person tends to uphold the value of autonomy and individuality, referred to as "selfing," not just for themselves but also for their partner. For them, love means choosing to create powerful lives separately and coming together from a space of choice.

Those who tend toward "selfing" are really good at expressing what they want and need. They are clear on what they believe. They assert their selfhood. For them, love looks like tuning into what you want and being willing to represent that to another. It looks like speaking your mind, no matter what.

To some, this way of being might come off as and feel selfish—like self-absorption empathic awareness. For example, they might go into the kitchen to get a drink, and it never crosses their mind to get one for their partner. That a lack of consciousness can lead to conflict.

On the other hand, those who tend toward "othering" are more empathic. They are inclined to tune into others' needs and feelings very well, but are less skilled at "selfing." For them, love looks like taking care of others, sometimes to their own detriment.

In truth, both are right.

Most conflicts arise when one partner feels unimportant, or is not receiving enough connection, time, or love from the other. While this desire for togetherness serves the relationship itself—the "Sacred Third" entity—it can turn into a shadow aspect if driven by anxiety stemming from a lack of self-connection.

For the individualist, or "selfer," the challenge lies in staying present with the physical sensations that arise in moments of intense communion. This intensity often prompts them to retreat and seek calm on their own.

Ironically, what makes the "selfer" feel safe—time alone—can make the other feel disconnected, abandoned, and afraid. Conversely, the need to connect—wanting to "hug it out" or talk it through— provides comfort for the "otherer," but can make the "selfer" feel smothered and panicked.

In truth, both partners need a balance of these approaches to create a healthy relationship.

Typically, one partner excels at "selfing" and the other at "othering," each coming together to cross-train their partner's less developed skill.

This mutual growth is, at its core, why people are drawn to each other.

The "selfer" knows, even if unconsciously, that something in them feels incomplete. They long for connection but often protect their independence above all else. The "otherer" also feels incomplete in a different way—seeking wholeness through closeness, sometimes at the expense of their own needs or clarity.

Like the two hemispheres of the brain, these relational tendencies are designed to complement one another. Full functionality and optimal relating require both: individuality and connection, self-awareness and attunement, personal truth and shared experience. In a healthy relationship, the "selfer" and "otherer" learn to cross-train—

by developing the less dominant muscle in the other. Over time, the "selfer" becomes more relationally receptive, and the "otherer" becomes more self-referencing and boundaried. This is what Growing Together looks like in real time.

Where it gets tricky is when you're upset and when you are unconscious of these dynamics, the reactions to lovelessness, interpreted in whichever way you perceive it, pull you into your default. And when you are unaware of these dynamics, you interpret any disruption in the flow of love through your particular lens:

- The "selfer": experiencing closeness as pressure, may interpret it as suffocation.
- The "otherer": experiencing distance as abandonment, may interpret it as rejection.

The "selfer" then retreats to avoid being engulfed—and ends up alone. The "otherer" grasps to avoid being abandoned—and ends up pushed away. In both cases, you create the very reality you fear most.

Herein lies a pivot point where another way forward is possible. One that interrupts the old patterns of anxiety, fear, blame, guilt, shame, criticism, and judgment. One that asks you to bring conscious attention not to the conflict at hand, but to the Sacred Third—the relationship itself, the living space between you. Even when the situation hasn't changed and your partner is still triggered or the dynamic feels stuck, your perspective can shift. And that willingness to see things differently is what changes everything.

Rather than shutting down, you choose to stay open. Rather than collapsing into acquiescence, you remain curious. Rather than disconnecting, you choose to remain present. And even though the conflictual situation may not have changed, your perspective on it does—growing capacity, building trust, creating a place where both connection and autonomy are welcome. It is from your willingness to stay with it that you can use conflict as a crucible for growth.

THINGS LEFT UNSAID

> Between what is said and not meant, and what is meant and not
> said, most of love is lost.
>
> — KAHLIL GIBRAN

There will be times in your relationship when words need to be
spoken, thoughts shared, beliefs revealed, and true desires—those
you've been keeping safely tucked away—brought into the open, often
when you least feel ready. In fact, the idea of experiencing that level of
vulnerability by uttering your words aloud can feel like you're about
to die.

It is in the Growing Together stage that the work you did to Grow
yourself Down, to upgrade your own personal IOS, gets to be used in
service of upgrading the operating system of your Sacred Third.

You might know what it's like to let time pass while things go
unspoken. The situation doesn't resolve—it just lives inside you,
quietly growing into greater anxiety, uncertainty, doubt, frustration, or
even anger.

Not talking—a lie of omission—just creates more awkwardness
and tension in a relationship than necessary. (If you think the other

person is oblivious to this, you're wrong. Think of times when you knew something was up even when the other person said nothing. You can sense it by their eyes, the feel of their handshake or hug or touch, or the tone of their voice.)

Tough challenges don't go away, but they are often difficult to talk about.

According to the book, *Difficult Conversations: How to Discuss What Matters Most,* by Bruce Patton, Douglas Stone, and Sheila Heen, the three most significant errors people make in conversations (or lack thereof) are:

- Assuming you know what happened, what should happen, and who is to blame.
- Hiding your feelings (or letting them loose in ways you later regret).
- Interpreting the situation as a reflection of your identity or self-worth.[21]

Avoiding these mistakes isn't easy.

It's important to shift your thinking from "I need to explain/justify myself" to "I need to listen and learn more about what's going on, and to do so with courage and an open heart." The key to any difficult (or courageous) conversation is **preparation.**

The Love Lab Challenge: What are the things you have been hesitant to share? Been left unsaid? Things you are still carrying around longer than comfortable? Take the first step of sharing by giving yourself permission to write them out. By no means are you obligated to share this with another until you are ready. At the very least, use this exercise to gain more clarity about shifting the pattern of withholding for yourself. If nothing else, there is such value in creating greater awareness.

- What are YOU thinking and feeling (what are the stories you are telling yourself about the situation/person)?
- What are the things that have been left unsaid, and why?
- Open your heart: Put yourself in the other person's shoes— if you were them, what might you be thinking and feeling but not saying?

Taking the time to understand both perspectives prior to engaging in a conversation is the best preparation for a heartfelt outcome in service of your Sacred Third.

INTIMACY AND COLLABORATION

A generous heart is always open, always ready to receive our going and coming. In the midst of such love we need never fear abandonment. This is the most precious gift true love offers—the experience of knowing we always belong.

— BELL HOOKS

Unless you are a psychopath, intimacy and collaboration are what we most crave. From cradle to grave, we navigate life seeking connection. Being willing to engage in difficult conversations repeatedly, even when socialized conditioning might have you retreat into silence, is one of the most powerful skills you will ever master.

My clients learn the skills needed to stay connected to their partner in a step-by-step way, despite myriad challenges that may arise. They know the value of responsibility, curiosity, honesty, genuineness, and sincerity—and act on it.

It's a powerful stand for Love.

When a relationship is in conflict, it's because it's lopsided: too much in/out breath and not enough of the other. Either you are not connecting enough, or you are too jammed up together. Conflict then becomes a means to either:

- Give the relationship a break and be separate; or
- Call it together because everyone's been doing their own thing.

When two different perspectives try to connect unsuccessfully, the result isn't just tension—it's a failed attempt at collaboration. Both people end up in conflict, not directly with each other but with a third thing, *a misunderstanding*.

At the core of that misunderstanding is a deeper truth neither is quite saying: "I don't feel heard, seen, understood, respected." And when you boil it all way down, what's often underneath is this: "I don't feel loved right now" and "I don't matter to you."

But that is an illusion.

Most couples I work with haven't stopped loving one another. Love is still there. It's the very thing that is funding the drama. If neither cared for nor loved one another, why fight?

There are two dynamics that interfere with intimacy, with your ability to come together, to collaborate, and to re-return adopting the perspective of "US" in service of the Sacred Third: coercion and collapse.

Coercion is any way that intends to threaten, punish, withhold love, or dangle something to get your partner to do what you want. It's a conscious manipulation—the emotional version of putting a gun to someone's head and placing a partner in a double bind: If they stand for what they want, they're going to lose something they value.

Collapse occurs when, in an effort to avoid conflict or maintain peace, you relinquish your own perspective. It's that moment when two differing views come together, and rather than stay true to what matters to you, you shrink back. You may say, "Fine, I don't have to do what I was planning. It's cool but inside you've buried your desire, need, want, or truth way down.

The troubling thing about collapse is that you don't actually let it go—you just go quiet. Over time, resentments build, accumulating like termites that eat at the foundation of a house. And one day, out of the blue, the whole relationship is bound to come crashing down.

It's impossible to build a structure on a foundation riddled with holes.

That being said, conflict is not just all doom and gloom. It actually has its own unique intelligence intended to allow for dissolution of what is not working, so a new level of relational strength is allowed to grow.

Conflict has a developmental utility to it.

~

The Love Lab Challenge: Building on things left unsaid, let's have you now tend to your piece of the Red Thread in service of your Sacred Third. Take one hundred percent responsibility for your part of the relationship dynamic. Answer the following inquiries as a way to gain more clarity and use what you learn to create a starting point for a conversation that becomes collaborative.

- How are you meant to prepare to share the things you've left unsaid, so you are both tending to the care and feeding of your Relationship?
- What is funding your grumbling?
- How do you collude with conflict by coercion or collapse?
- What is your one hundred percent responsibility of fifty percent of the conflict?

ALIVENESS: THE ANTIDOTE TO DEATH

Let's be in awe which doesn't mean anything but the courage to gape like fish at the surface breaking around our mouths as we meet the air.

— MARK NEPO

Commitment in a relationship is not just about staying together; it's about elevating the way you show up for yourself and for each other. It's about being in a consistent practice of upgrading your own personal IOS so that your relationship is a sanctuary for the heart and a springboard for your mutual dreams.

True commitment begins with self-awareness. You have to know what you're bringing into the relationship—the patterns, habits, and emotional responses you've learned over the years—all the exploration that were part of your Growing Down and Growing Up process. When you finally commit to a relationship, you're not just committing to your partner, you're committing to the highest version of yourself. You're saying, "I'm here to grow, evolve, and support us both in creating the most beautiful life possible together."

Relationships are like mirrors. They reflect both the beauty and the unresolved parts of us that need attention. When you elevate your IOS, you consciously choose to face those reflections with compassion and curiosity rather than fear and defensiveness. You transform challenges into opportunities to deepen intimacy. Each trigger becomes a doorway, not to disconnection but rather to greater understanding and alignment. The ability to take multiple perspectives creates greater ease in Love. It is why we need our partner.

You can see in one area, not in another. Your partner can see your blind spots. It's akin to you being able to see in the light, and they can see in the dark. Their genius helps you. If you want someone to choose a life with you, they must feel *alive* with you.

What do I mean by aliveness?

Aliveness is the willingness to feel all your feelings—all eighty-eight keys of your emotional keyboard—to breathe into and be present with them no matter how challenging they may be. Your partner is looking to feel safe with theirs—they're looking for a refuge.

In order to be that refuge, you have to be able to be with your own feelings. When you bring it down to the basics, feelings are just a matrix of physical sensations in the body—like hunger or an itch. Our bodies give us indications all the time. Feelings are different from the STORY we have about the feelings, from the meaning we create.

When a feeling arises in you, how do you respond? Is it welcome? Or not? When it arises in your partner, how do you respond? Is it welcome? Or not?

Imagine your relationship as a sacred container, one where your vulnerabilities are met with kindness, your desires are honored and celebrated, and your growth is nurtured. This kind of relationship requires BOTH partners to commit to ongoing self-inquiry, to sharpening their emotional intelligence, and elevate how they communicate and co-create.

It is also about attention—about noticing all of the ways in which your partner expresses their "I love you's" without actually saying it: flowers left on the dining room table, warming of a car in below-freezing temperatures, cooking of a favorite meal, opening of a door, holding of hands, and noticing you're tired and quietly making your favorite tea, placing it beside you without fanfare.

Power is the ability to direct your attention in order to be able to better see all the nuanced and overt ways in which the hidden "I love you's" are expressed. Noticing the smuggled "I love you's" and sharing them in return builds your Sacred Third Relationship bank account—like small, consistent deposits from which you can withdraw.

When your relationship is rooted in elevated consciousness, it becomes a sanctuary where you both feel safe to be fully seen and loved. But it's also a launchpad—a place from which you both leap toward your dreams, knowing you have each other's unwavering support.

This is where love transforms from something you have, to something you *are*.

Together, you're no longer just surviving life; you're thriving, building a Legacy of Love that impacts everything you touch.

~

The Love Lab Challenge: What are the ways in which your partner expresses their love for you without saying it? Power lies in the ability to direct your attention to those small, seemingly insignificant gestures that speak volumes: emptying the dishwasher, washing your car, or picking up a wet towel.

Begin to build a practice of tracking these unspoken, smuggled acts of caring for you and acknowledge your partner for them with an appreciative "I noticed that you … thank you …. It made me feel loved and taken care of."

PURPOSEFUL COMMUNICATION

Say what's true—not to be right, but to be genuine.

— JOËLLE LYDON

Your relationship, when applying the Sacred Third perspective, is a living, breathing entity with its own characteristics, personality, and shortcomings. If everything is running smoothly, the experience of being together feels effortless, like you're gliding on a gentle current together. When challenges arise (and they will—remember? You chose them for their crazy...!), it can feel like you're navigating choppy waters, trying to miss boulders and the impending waterfall.

Here's where consistent and ongoing relational bank deposits in the form of acknowledged acts of "I love you's" and purposeful communications come into play—troubles are not just speed bumps, but golden opportunities to elevate and refine the way you connect. They create more navigational certainty. You can use these moments to either tear each other and your relationship down or transform and strengthen your bond.

Research from psychologist Dr. John Gottman, PhD, highlights that couples who face challenges with empathy and openness tend to build stronger, more resilient relationships.[22] Harville Hendrix, with his Imago Relationship Therapy[23] framework, shares that conflicts often bring unresolved issues to the surface, so you may work on them while healing and growing as a couple. Dr. Sue Johnson, known for her work in Emotional Focused Therapy (EFT),[24] shares that when handled with intention and love, difficult conversations make relationships stronger and more supportive.

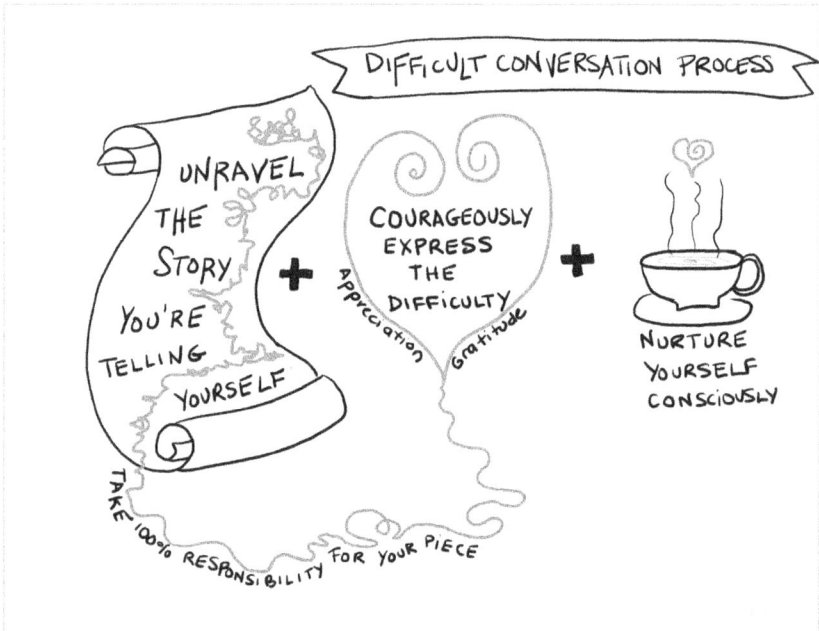

Here's the truth: If you choose to be in a relationship, conflicts arise. They will never not go away. Nor are they something to avoid. Lean into conflicts with a heart full of curiosity and care. They invite a deeper level of understanding and connection.

When conflict arises, it's a sign that something no longer works—whether that be a pattern of behavior or thought, a dynamic, or even an expectation. In that moment, your relationship is being invited to adapt and grow.

Instead of seeing these moments as an affront or something to avoid, lean in:

1. First, own your piece of the Red Thread, regulate your nervous system, and unravel the story you are telling yourself about the situation.
2. Express the difficulty with honesty, appreciation, and gratitude.
3. Tend to yourself.

This ongoing approach to difficulty will have you positioned to consistently keep Growing Together as a couple.

Just watch out for complacent thinking: "I've mastered this relationship thing. We're good." Just like plants, relationships require continual care. If you stop tending to them, they will wither. The intention is to keep growing. Even a master gardener pays attention to the seasons, the needs of each plant, and the soil in which it grows. Seeding, maintaining, pruning, controlled burns, propagation, and regeneration. Your relational landscape is always evolving.

This is how the real work happens—moving from unconscious incompetence to unconscious mastery until your new relational way of being becomes second nature.

This is how you get to, choice by choice, step by step, leave a Legacy of Love.

EVERYDAY PRACTICE OF LOVE

The impatient idealist says: "Give me a place to stand and I shall move the earth." But such a place does not exist. We all have to stand on the earth itself and go with her at her pace.

— CHINUA ACHEBE

With trust as your new normal, and commitment to stand for Love, friction and conflict are not traumas but opportunities in your relationship. Redefining those sticky areas between you as new challenges to work on allows your relationship to continue to evolve and grow into its next iteration, delivering the upgrade you both signed up for by committing to one another.

Just as we bathe regularly to maintain healthy hygiene, it's imperative you consistently work on these steps again and again for healthy mental and emotional hygiene in your relationship. It's not about going back to the beginning each time or repeating first grade. It's about moving to advanced levels of inner trust, both individually and interdependently, so that your choices and actions align with the evolving needs of your relationship.

This is the path of relational mastery. Not to perceive conflict, challenge, or difficulty as a problem. Instead, see it as a signal.

Imagine conflict in a relationship as a visit to the gym. You can have a membership and the intention to go several times a week, but just showing up sporadically leaves you disappointed when you don't get the results you wanted. Similarly, expecting a relationship to be free of conflict can cause you to slip into outdated ways of functioning—only to beat yourself up for falling prey to the same old patterns, again.

If you approach the "conflict gym" with consciousness and a commitment to deliberate practices, you begin to build resilience. Just as lifting weights causes micro-tears in the muscles, which heal and grow back stronger, relationships also need these small disruptions to cause strength and resilience over time.

Conflict, like a workout, is not a negative thing. It transforms your relationship into a more robust, harmonious partnership, just as gym workouts create a stronger physical body. It's developmentally useful, so both partners can alchemize to better understand one another over the long-term.

The myth of happily ever after is often put on a pedestal. We're conditioned to chase it like a prize, thinking it's the ultimate measure of a successful life or relationship. However, the opposite of being dead *isn't* being happy—it's being **alive**. The point of being in love isn't to create a constant state of bliss; it's to expand, to grow, to push the edges of who we are and how we relate with one another. If you're always measuring your real, imperfect love against some idealized version of romance—something out of a fairy-tale or movie plot—you'll never feel truly satisfied.

Real love, the kind that's rooted in the everyday, in the messy and beautiful complexities of attachment, doesn't look like a highlight reel. It's full of negotiation, vulnerability, and the gritty work of showing up for each other.

When you compare your relationship to some fantasy of how it "should" be, you reject the messy but genuine love you already have. You're essentially saying, "I want something different, something perfect." But perfection isn't possible—not with this or any other person, in this or any other moment, given the very real circumstances of your life.

The reality you're living is the best possible outcome, given where you are in your own growth, where your partner is, and where your relationship stands. Wishing it were different is like picking a fight with the Universe, and that's a battle you'll lose every single time. Instead of trading in real, grounded love for an unattainable fantasy, choose what's in front of you. Embrace it fully.

See your relationship as the very best version of what you and your partner can create together at this moment. When you choose to stay, to nurture, and to grow within your relationship, you're not just building a bond—you're creating a Legacy of Love. One that can ripple out, influencing those around you and carrying forward to future generations.

So, the next time you're in the thick of it—when you're arguing on a random Wednesday afternoon and thinking, *"This doesn't feel like love,"* remember this:

> "This is what real love looks like. Sometimes it's messy, confus- ing, heartbreaking, and intense. But our love is bigger than this moment, stronger than this argument. Together, we'll find our way through. My job, right now, is to breathe, to find a place of calm, to open my heart (even though it wants to shut down), and to remember my own worth. And then to remember—even though they might be driving me crazy right now—how amazing this person truly is."

That's where real, lasting love lives—in the choice to stay present, to stay open, to see the humanity and innocence in your partner and in yourself, even when things get tough. And in that choice, you're not just shaping your relationship; you're creating a powerful Legacy of Love that will endure far beyond today's momentary challenges.

∽

Creative Edge Experience: What We Feed Grows—A Collaborative Collage. Your rela- tionship is a living entity. It responds to what you give it—time, attention, presence, love, and care. Get clear about the energies you most want to cultivate in your Sacred Third, and explore how, day by day, our choices either water those seeds or leave them to dry.

You'll need:

- A sheet of plain paper or poster board
- A few old magazines
- Scissors and a glue stick
- Markers or pens

Follow these steps:

1. Attune together. Quietly drop in and ask yourself: *What do I want more of in our relationship? What qualities, experiences, or energies feel vital with the "US" that we are growing?* Write three to five words or phrases that arise.

2. Gather images. Intuitively flip through the magazines, cutting images and words that you each want to cultivate— let your hands lead more than your head.

3. Create. On your paper/board, decide whether a garden or a tree (or another image) is the most aligned with your relationship and collaborate to create it—remembering these are metaphors for growth, care, and thriving. Arrange and glue down your images or words.

4. Nutrients. Use your markers to draw or write the daily nutrients your relationship needs to grow. For example: *Daily check-ins.* Let this be collaborative.

5. Reflect and share. When your collage feels complete, sit with it and each other and reflect on where you feel invited to take more responsibility for the care of your Sacred Third. Agree on one practice you will recommit to in the upcoming week.

LEAVING A LEGACY OF LOVE

> *One regret, dear world,*
> *That I am determined not to have*
> *When I am lying on my deathbed*
> *Is that*
> *I did not kiss you enough.*
>
> — HAFIZ

Deep breath.

As we near the end of this journey together—and before we take one more step—I want to pause. Not because there isn't more to do but because learning to pause is the work. I want you to tap into the incredible power of slowing down long enough to truly receive the shifts that have already begun to be created. To acknowledge all the willingness, courage, and commitment you've shown—especially when it tested your resolve. Especially when it would have been so much easier and simpler to skip over the tough parts and default to old ways of operating.

Before I offer you the next steps to keep the momentum we've built together going, I want you to see yourself. One of the reasons you may have struggled in your relationships—finding yourself repeating patterns of suffering—is because the same skills that built your career (quick thinking, pushing, moving fast, being nimble) have become your default.

Slowing down feels impossible.

A luxury.

Something you brush aside as you rush on to the next thing.

But here's the truth: When you don't create space to reflect and digest, acknowledging even the smallest of shifts, you rob yourself of the fuel and fortification real growth needs. Your brain doesn't register the change as real. And without realizing, you slip back into the cycles you've just spent this entire book liberating yourself from.

When you pause, you anchor the change in your heart, body, mind, and spirit. You feel the shifts—and become them. And from that grounded place, you begin to make different choices—ones that support your ongoing growth. That being said, before we move forward, take one final, short pause to digest what's shifted by reflecting on the questions below.

〜

The Love Lab Challenge: Use the sentence starter provided—yes, really write the answers down:

- What changes have you started to see that make you proud? I am proud that …

- What have you let go of? What have you let in? I acknowledge I've let go of … I acknowledge I've let in …

- What have you learned about yourself, how you operate, and what you need? I've learned that I …

- What patterns were you blind to—or didn't have the words to describe—before? I can now see that ...

- What wisdom do you want to remember? I know that ...

Well done.
Acknowledge how you've grown since we began. Let it land.

⁓

My role has been to create structures and experiences for those of you with the courage and willingness to relate differently. For those committed to honoring both your intellect and your intuition, expanding your mind while opening your heart—and creating relationship possibilities beyond what you currently know.

My work is to build a container for you to:

- Root into clarity;
- Build your new relationship baseline;
- Rewrite your inner story;
- Trust the compass within;
- Honor your sacred boundaries;
- Navigate difficulty with grace;
- And expand your Legacy of Love.

Know this: As you prepare to bring what you've learned into your relationships, it's normal to feel wobbly sometimes. It's normal to want support. You're not alone. Resources for connecting with me are listed in the resources section—you are always welcome to reach out for a Discovery Session with me. I would love to hear how your journey continues to unfold.

And now, one final reflection.

Personally, I have come a very long way from that moment of surrender in the psych ward all those years ago—that line-in-the-sand decision not to carry my formative baggage to the grave. Since then, more lines have been drawn. Each one bringing sharper clarity around my purpose and my calling.

The healing began with me—untangling old patterns, upgrading my own IOS, learning to love differently. Soon it became more: a living, breathing model I could offer to my son. And while he walks his own unique path, he has told me more than once of his aspiration to create a relationship like the one he sees my husband and me nurturing together. That close to home intention became another threshold—one marked by faith: faith that this relational work could ripple outward into something larger than just my lifetime.

Could the work I do here touch the lives of his children? And their children? Seven generations forward? And could it ripple backward, too? Reaching the women and men who came before me—those who didn't have the tools, resources, or support to love on their own terms?

My heart believes it can. Does yours?

As Maya Angelou once shared with Oprah: *"Legacy is every life you touch."*

This means that every small action matters. Every repaired conversation. Every moment you stay when it would be easier to walk away. Every time you choose tenderness over winning, connection over control.

This is what it means to leave a Legacy of Love.

Not one day. Not once you've "done the work" and perfected yourself. Here, now, in your relationships. Every. Single. Day.

Supporting others in stepping into that choice expands not only our sense of responsibility to one another, it expands our devotion to this beautiful planet we call home. To live with that kind of attention. That kind of intention.

That is the legacy you are being invited into. The one we get to create together.

RESOURCES

For your personal Love readiness assessment and to discover where you are on your path to cultivating a deep, thriving relationship: How Deep Are Your Roots Assessment: https://joellelydon.com/assessment

To learn more about Joëlle, her coaching and mentoring, personal and professional trainings, speaking, programs, and workshops, visit: https://joellelydon.com/.

Subscribe to Weekly Love Notes: http://eepurl.com/dOmisb.

To apply for a 60-minute confidential Discovery Session with Joëlle: www.TheDiscoverySession.com.

REFERENCES
REFERENCED BOOKS AND WEBSITE LINKS

Redfield, James. *Celestine Prophecy*. Boston, MA: Little, Brown & Co, 1994.

Thomashauer, Regena. *Pussy: A Reclamation*. Hay House, 2017.

Campbell, Joseph. *The Hero with a Thousand Faces: A Brilliant Examination, Through Ancient Hero Myths, of Man's Eternal Struggle for Identity*. Nueva York: Fontana Press, 1949.

Anne Davin. http://www.AnneDavin.com/.

A Course in Miracles. Tiburon: Foundation for Inner Peace, 1975-, 1975.

Maltz, Maxwell. *Psycho-Cybernetics: The Original Text of the Classic Guide to a New Life*. New York: Penguin Publishing Group, 2016.

Cloud, Henry. *9 Things a Leader Must Do*. Nashville, Tenn: Thomas Nelson, 2006.

Hendricks, Gay. *The Big Leap*. New York, NY: HarperCollins, 2009.

Siegel, Daniel J., and Tina Payne Bryson. *The Whole-Brain Child: 12 Revolutionary Strategies to Nurture Your Child's Developing Brain*. Los Angeles, CA: Mind Your Brain, Inc., 2013.

Love is a Battlefield. Pat Benatar. RCA, n.d., 1983.

Brown, Brené. *Daring Greatly: How the Courage to be Vulnerable Transforms the Way We Live, Love, Parent, and Lead*. London: Penguin Books Ltd, 2018.

Williamson, Marianne. *A Return to Love: Reflections on the Principles of a Course in Miracles*. New York, NY: HarperOne, 2012.

"Center for Intentional Creativity." MUSEA. https://musea.org.

Ruiz, Miguel. *The Four Agreements: A Toltec Wisdom Book*. San Rafael: Amber-Allen Pub, 1997.

Stone, Douglas, Bruce Patton, and Sheila Heen. *Difficult Conversations: How to Discuss What Matters Most*. London: Portfolio/Penguin, 2011.

Gottman, John Mordechai, and Nan Silver. *The Seven Principles for Making Marriage Work*. London: Orion Spring, 2023.

"Annie Lalla - Love Coach for Singles & Couples." AnnieLalla.com. https://www.annielalla.com/.

Hendrix, Harville, and Helen Hunt. *Getting the Love You Want: A Guide for Couples*. New York: Henry Holt and Company, 2022.

Johnson, Susan M. *Hold Me Tight: Seven Conversations for a Lifetime of Love*. New York: Little, Brown Spark, 2020.

Hübl, Thomas, and Julie Jordan Avritt. *Attuned: Practicing Interdepen-

dence to Heal Our Trauma-and Our World. Boulder, CO: Sounds True, 2023.

Turner, Toko-pa. *Belonging: Remembering Ourselves Home*. Salt Spring Island, British Columbia: Her Own Room Press, 2019.

ENDNOTES

1. "The Red String of Fate." Medium, February 1, 2023. https://medium.com/@safofive/the-red-string-of-fate-acd26c61bd1f.
2. The Insight of Interbeing - Garrison Institute. https://www.garrisoninstitute.org/insight-of-interbeing/.
3. McCloud, Shiloh Sophia. *The Way of the Red Thread: Creating a Culture of Connection*. Cosmic Cowgirls Ink, LLC, n.d.
4. Ruiz, Miguel. *The Four Agreements: Toltec Wisdom Collection*. San Rafael, Calif: Amber-Allen Pub, 2008.
5. Training, Innovation. "The Four Stages of Competence Model - Innovation Training: Design." Innovation Training | Design Thinking Workshops, February 4, 2025. https://www.innovationtraining.org/the-four-stages-of-competence-model.
6. Rankin, Lissa. "How to Find Your Calling: Navigating Your Own Hero's Journey." explore deeply, January 11, 2024. https://exploredeeply.com/live-your-purpose/how-to-find-your-calling-navigating-your-own-heros-journey.
7. "Chapter 7.X: The Confusion of Pain and Joy: Acim." A

Course in Miracles. https://acim.org/acim/chapter-7/the-confusion-of-pain-and-joy/en/s/116.

8. Maltz, Maxwell. *Psycho-Cybernetics: The Original Text of the Classic Guide to a New Life*. New York: Penguin Publishing Group, 2016.

9. Beattie, Melody. *Beyond Codependency: Getting Better All the Time*. Hazelden Publishing, 2009.

10. Lighthorse, Pixie. *Boundaries and Protection*. ROW HOUSE PUB, 2025.

11. Chemaly, Soraya. *Rage Becomes Her: The Power of Women's Anger*. New York: Atria Paperback, an imprint of Simon & Schuster, Inc., 2019.

12. Cloud, Henry. *9 Things a Leader Must Do*. Nashville, Tenn: Thomas Nelson, 2006.

13. Hendricks, Gay. *The Big Leap*. New York, NY: HarperCollins, 2009.

14. Though the term "havingness" originated in Scientology teachings, it has since been widely adopted and reinterpreted by contemporary coaches, therapists, and embodiment teachers. Figures like Mama Gena, Layla Martin, Alex Howard, and Lauren Walsh use the term to describe a person's capacity to receive and sustain emotional nourishment, love, and success. Increasing one's "havingness" is a vital part of allowing deeper intimacy and holding more goodness without sabotage or shutdown.

15. Baraz, James, and Shoshana Alexander. "The Helper's High." Greater Good. 2010. https://greatergood.berkeley.edu/article/item/the_helpers_high.

16. Small, Angela. "The Power of Doodling: Enhancing Cognitive Abilities." 90.7 WKGC Public Media, May 3, 2024. https://www.wkgc.org/2024/05/03/the-power-of-doodling-enhancing-cognitive-abilities/.

17. By, Saul McLeod, Updated on, and April 20. "John Bowlby's Attachment Theory." Simply Psychology, April 20, 2025. https://www.simplypsychology.org/bowlby.html and "Mary

Ainsworth Strange Situation Experiment." Simply Psychology, May 20, 2025. https://www.simplypsychology.org/mary-ainsworth.html.

18. Siegel, Daniel J., and Tina Payne Bryson. *The Whole-Brain Child: 12 Revolutionary Strategies to Nurture Your Child's Developing Brain*. Los Angeles, CA: Mind Your Brain, Inc., 2013.

19. "Edge and Other Wildlife Concepts - Oklahoma State University." Edge and Other Wildlife Concepts | Oklahoma State University, April 1, 2017. https://extension.okstate.edu/fact-sheets/edge-and-other-wildlife-concepts.html.

20. Hendrix, Harville, and Helen Hunt. *Getting the Love You Want: A Guide for Couples*. New York: Henry Holt and Company, 2022.

21. "5 Steps for Tackling Difficult Conversations." CCL, May 8, 2025. https://www.ccl.org/articles/leading-effectively-articles/5-steps-for-tackling-tough-conversations/.

22. Lisitsa, Ellie. "Expressing Compassion and Empathy." The Gottman Institute, March 5, 2024. https://www.gottman.com/blog/what-makes-love-last-expressing-compassion-and-empathy/?utm_source=chatgpt.com.

23. "What Is Imago?" Harville Hendrix and Helen Hunt, March 15, 2022. https://harvilleandhelen.com/initiatives/what-is-imago/.

24. Treleaven, Sarah. "The Science behind Happy and Healthy Relationships." Time, June 26, 2018. https://time.com/5321262/science-behind-happy-healthy-relationships/?utm_source=chatgpt.com.

ACKNOWLEDGMENTS

It truly took a village to bring this book to life.

The pages you now hold would not exist without the hands, hearts, and spirits of so many. Each person offered a thread—essential, sacred, and unmistakably theirs. Without these threads, this journey would have been lonelier, slower, and far less joyful.

To my editor, Deborah Kevin—thank you for holding a clear and loving container each week, for offering wise, steady feedback, and for seeing the full vision of this book even before I could. Your presence made this process not only manageable but magical. Being a first-time author has been a delight.

To Lisa Hromada—thank you for the exquisite cover image. You translated the soul of this book into visual form with grace and accuracy, capturing something deeper than words.

To my husband, Matthew Schueler—my soul mate, best friend, and life partner. Your steadiness, humor, and fierce devotion have been the ground I've stood on again and again. Thank you for every single moment of encouragement, every pre-edit and pre-revision, every reminder that I could do this. Most of all, thank you for loving me the way you do. You make everything feel possible and worthwhile.

To my son, Liam Bader—you were worth the seven-year wait. You are the heartbeat behind this work, the living proof that love transforms.

Thank you for the privilege of choosing me as your Mama. Being your mother has cracked me wide open in the most sacred of ways and made me braver, softer, and stronger than I ever imagined possible.

Darline Turner—my soul sister, my Thursday morning mirror. Ten years of "spring cleanings," of holding and being held, of laughing, crying, becoming. You've witnessed it all. I am on my knees in gratitude.

To my family—my mother, my father, my sisters and brother—your love, named or unspoken, has informed the very shape of who I am. From this complex and potent lineage, I've drawn both the questions and the strength that have led me here. Thank you for being my Wayfinder kiosk.

To my dear friends—you know who you are—thank you for listening, again and again, as I prattled on about love and relationships, heartbreak and healing. Your patience with this adorable weirdo knows no bounds. Thank you for our impromptu drumming and singing circles, the boat rides, the painting parties, and dinners—all the ways you reminded me that joy, connection, and belly laughter are just as sacred as the work.

And finally, to the teachers and mentors who have lit the path ahead, called forth the most honest, grounded version of me—Debbie and Carlos Rosas, Regena Thomashauer, Kasia Urbaniak, Heather Dominick-Kosmicki, Annie Lalla, and Shiloh Sophia—thank you for your generosity, your heart, your fierce determination, and your unbounded love. You've challenged me, held me, believed in me, and modeled what it means to live, love, and lead with an unbreakable heart.

With every word, I carry your imprint.
    -JL

ABOUT THE AUTHOR

Photo credit: Andrew Elder

Joëlle Lydon is a certified relationship coach, author, educator, certified Intentional Creativity® teacher, and expressive arts facilitator who helps individuals and couples build deeply connected, emotionally intelligent relationships—at home and in life. Her work blends creativity, neuroscience, and personal development, empowering people to move beyond old patterns and into courageous, sustainable connection.

With over three decades of experience, Joëlle draws on her background as a public-school teacher and adjunct professor to bring presence, clarity, and strategy to her coaching. Since 1985, she's been in the business of building trust, cultivating connection, and helping people grow. Her signature frameworks offer a grounded, step-by-step path for transforming how we love, lead, and relate.

Born in England and raised internationally, Joëlle brings a global lens and deeply human approach to her work. Her own journey through mismatched partnerships, thriving love, and the support of coaches, mentors, and therapists led her to pioneer a holistic, creative methodology that supports both the inner and outer dimensions of relational growth.

When she's not guiding others through transformative 1-1 coaching, retreats or workshops, you'll find Joëlle savoring slow morning with tea on the patio, dancing Nia, painting for the joy of it, exploring the world with her beloved husband, Matthew, gathering with heart-expanding friends or napping beside her seventeen-year-old cat, Sake. To learn more about her work, visit her website.

linkedin.com/in/joellelydon
instagram.com/joellelydon

ABOUT THE PUBLISHER

Founded in 2019, Highlander Press is a vibrant, mid-sized publishing house dedicated to transforming the world through the power of words. We are deeply committed to diversity and bringing big ideas to the forefront. At Highlander Press, we help authors navigate the journey from initial concept through writing, editing, and publishing, culminating in the release of a book that not only fulfills a lifelong dream but also solidifies their expertise and boosts their confidence.

Our unique approach centers on forging strong, collaborative relationships with women-owned businesses across the publishing spectrum, including graphic design, marketing, launching, copyright management, and publicity. We believe in the power of community and operate by the mantra, "a rising tide lifts all boats." This philosophy not only enhances our business model but also ensures that our authors receive unparalleled support and opportunities to succeed.

Join us in making a mark in the literary world, where your voice is heard, and your message has the power to change lives.

facebook.com/highlanderpress
instagram.com/highlanderpress
linkedin.com/company/highlander-press

www.ingramcontent.com/pod-product-compliance
Lightning Source LLC
Chambersburg PA
CBHW052019030426
42335CB00026B/3208